Jobs for All

Jobs for All

Capitalism on Trial

PAUL HELLYER

 METHUEN

Toronto   New York   London   Sydney   Auckland

Canadian Cataloguing in Publication Data

Hellyer, Paul, 1923–
  Jobs for all

Bibliography: p.
ISBN 0-458-97410-2

1. Unemployment—Canada—Effect of inflation on.
2. Canada—Economic policy.   I. Title.

HD5728.H44 1984   331.13'7971   C83-099303-7

Cover design: The Dragon's Eye Press

Printed and bound in Canada

1 2 3 4   84   88 87 86 85

To Ellen

without whom any contribution I have

made to public life would have been

impossible

Contents

But words are things, and a small drop of ink,

   Falling like dew, upon a thought, produces

That which makes thousands, perhaps millions think...

LORD BYRON

Acknowledgments

I would like to express my sincere appreciation to various people who helped in the preparation of this book.

My thanks to D. Campbell (Cam) Fraser, Catherine (Theresa) Day and Nancy Weiser for their painstaking assistance with the research; to Bill Bussiere, Gilbert (Gib) Parent, Vida Watson and my daughter Mary Elizabeth for reading the manuscript and pointing out areas in need of clarification for the lay reader; to Greg Cable for his general guidance and to Betty Corson for her most thoughtful and sensitive editing.

I am also grateful to Doug Peters and one or two other well-known economists. While they made many helpful and useful suggestions, they are in no way responsible for the heresies that are mine alone. Nor are they associated in any way with my sweeping indictment of mainline economists, which is not personal but simply a cris-de-coeur to the professionals to re-examine their beliefs in the light of the evidence around them.

Finally, may I tip my hat to those people who patiently typed drafts at various stages. They will be pleased to know that the word processor we had planned to use is finally on its way.

Preface

When I entered federal politics at the tender age of twenty-five there was widespread concern lest we suffer another depression like that of the wicked '30s. An economic maverick from my university days, I was motivated by the unshakable conviction that recessions and depressions reflect the folly of man and that they are readily avoidable. So I joined the action to help prevent a recurrence.

I was blithely unaware that neophyte MPs enjoy scant opportunity to alter the course of anything much of significance, but this gap in my understanding was more than offset by the intervention of the Korean war. It salvaged the situation, and talk of renewed depression soon faded. Later the postwar adoption of Keynesian economics shattered old shibboleths and ushered in an era of economic growth and stability.

A few years later I detected the embryo of a new problem in the growing concentration of power in big business and big labor. As early as 1961, in a keynote address to the Young Liberals at Banff, I warned my party of the potential threat to economic equilibrium. The seeds of inflation were being sown. Not surprisingly the warning fell on deaf ears. We were basking in the post-Korean glow and both unemployment and inflation were minuscule by current standards. Consequently, it was like the early diagnosis of a complicated disease before any of the visible symptoms become apparent.

You can't see it and don't want to talk about it in the fond hope that it will just go away.

But it didn't go away, and by 1969 the damaging effects of unregulated market power were much more evident. In the report of the Task Force on Housing and Urban Development we noted the small but menacing black cloud of inflation visible on the horizon. It was outside our terms of reference, but the Task Force urged the government to consider the threat as a matter of urgency because inflation could have a more negative effect on the affordability of housing than the combined positive effect of all the myriad recommendations to three levels of government and the construction industry. Again the caution was ignored.

Imagine my dismay a couple of years later when the government's belated action on the inflation front was limited to the discredited "tight money" approach. My patience snapped at the sight of hundreds of helpless constituents losing their jobs and self-respect—quite unnecessarily. I resigned from caucus and began the elusive search for allies concerned and compassionate enough to listen.

The quest led me to form Action Canada, the populist movement dedicated to full employment and zero inflation as a prerequisite to the resolution of other quality of life issues; then to the Progressive Conservative Party, where there was interest briefly, but only temporarily, as the more traditional elements moved inexorably toward their own special brand of Reaganomics; and finally back to the Liberal Party where the young people, at least, are searching for the essence of liberalism in the context of an unprecedented situation.

The urgency should be obvious. The economic upheaval of the late '70s and early '80s was more devastating than anyone could have imagined. It was totally inconsistent with a civilized society and tolerated only because a complacent majority were largely unaffected for so long. Little wonder that on January 5, 1983, the Canadian Conference of Catholic Bishops felt obliged to issue their *Ethical Reflections on the Economic Crisis* branding the unconscionable unemployment as morally untenable.

Those of us who escaped the ravages were just lucky that the central bankers turned off their doomsday machines before total disaster struck. Instead of collapsing the monetary system, they opened the sluice just in time to float a modest recovery.

The speed and the extent of recovery have been limited and will be restricted for years to come by the fact that the market-power disease remains. It wasn't cured by the near-lethal dose of sadistic monetarism, but merely suppressed. The virus lives on to strike again. That is the reason that inflation, and consequently interest rates, are too high to permit full employment policies, with the result that millions of people will be denied one of the most basic of human rights: the right to gainful employment.

On the value of human work and its place in creation I am in complete accord with the Bishops. The right to gainful employment should be as fundamental as freedom of speech. Still, our views diverge sharply on the means by which full employment at useful pursuits can be achieved. Unlike them, I believe that the current malaise is the child of human error rather than a fundamental weakness in the system. Furthermore, I am convinced that workers can enjoy a greater degree of freedom and dignity under liberal democracy than under any of the alternatives the Bishops might propose.

Jobs for all, and without insidious inflation, is a practical possibility. That's been my lifelong message. The pursuit of this ideal has been a long and convoluted journey—in its tortuous way my own personal marathon of hope. The race should have ended long ago, but must continue while health permits and the current sense of hopelessness demands.

This book marks the beginning of a new lap. It is my contribution to the dialogue the Bishops have called for. It is also a guidebook for Liberals who wonder what went wrong and where we should turn in the quest for relevance—a liberal manifesto, if you will.

It is my passionate wish that the Liberal Party, about which I feel so deeply and which I served so long, will take up the challenge. It has become increasingly uneasy as the unwitting handmaiden of big business, big labor, and big government. Instead, it should direct its attention to the hopes and aspirations of the young, the weak and the dispossessed—its real challenge and raison d'être.

1

Capitalism on Trial

Capitalism is on trial! That is the clear implication of the Bishops' *Ethical Reflections*. It is history repeating itself. Most of the serious charges laid in the "Dirty Thirties" were subsequently dropped because the system worked so superbly for so long in the post – World War II years. But the advent of stagflation raised new doubts, and the current unacceptable levels of unemployment have brought fresh indictments for crimes against God and humanity.

There is no denying the evidence of private capitalism's rocky record. From the early days of the Industrial Revolution, the output of goods has alternated between exhilarating highs and depressing lows. Each new advance brought new hope. But when the cycle turned down, controversy erupted with the predictability of Yellowstone Park's Old Faithful. Economists learned to accept cycles as endemic to the system. Like trees in the forest that grew in summer and lay dormant in winter, the periodic slumps were simply natural rest periods—plateaus from which the next ascent would be launched.

The confusion between natural and artificial phenomena has persisted for generations. Note has been taken of the cycle of fat and lean years in agriculture dating back as far as Joseph's exile in Egypt. Any good farmer knows that you have to make hay when the sun shines—in more ways than one.

The significance of cycles is accepted in the fashion industry, which, in contrast to agriculture, has the ability to create its own. Through a notorious abuse of planned obsolescence, manufacturers generate sales by adopting a rhythm of changes from wide lapels to narrow, high necklines to low, vivid shades to muted, and long skirts to mini-teasers. Style-conscious men and women are forced to keep buying in order to appear contemporary.

But neither the vagaries of the weather nor the whims of the couturier can adequately account for the wild fluctuations in output and employment in a diversified economy. These undulations can only be attributed to something much more elusive.

Karl Marx was completely disillusioned with the human consequences of the business cycles he observed. He saw that capitalists extracted the maximum of effort from their workers when business was expanding and then chopped them off the payroll like so many ripe cabbages when markets were saturated. The capitalists lived in luxury while it was always feast or famine for the hapless souls who really created the wealth.

Marx accused the owners of deliberate overproduction in order to establish and maintain oppressive power over the workers. The pool of unemployed and hungry labor helped to keep wages down. In this way the few gained at the expense of the many in accordance with M.I.T. Professor Lester Thurow's zero sum theory, which states that when someone gains economically it is likely to be at someone else's expense. Marx's moral outrage at the apparent unfairness prompted him to throw out the baby with the bathwater. He rejected the system as morally untenable and devised his own version of theoretically perfect Utopian socialism.

Like the classical economists who had influenced him, Marx was insufficiently perceptive to identify the abhorrent business cycles as monetary phenomena. It wasn't to grind labor into submission that led capitalists to lay off workers periodically. It was the fact that they couldn't sell all they could produce. And the shortage of customers wasn't related to need, which was great, but to the shortage of cash. The quantity of money in the system was independent of the supply of goods and services, so there was often insufficient demand to clear the market. Consequently, production was cut back and the cycle turned down.

The extreme test of this sad truth and its debilitating consequences came with the monetary contraction of the late 1920s and the great depression it produced. Seldom in recorded history has the ignorance of the few inflicted so much damage on the many.

It is a tribute to man's conservative nature that the mass suffering didn't lead to universal revolution. Perhaps the knowledge that the hardship was world-wide convinced sufferers that the pestilence was beyond man's control. A dash of residual puritanism helped the faithful to accept the plague as God's judgment on a wayward civilization bedeviled by speakeasies and Charleston girls.

Whatever the reason, it is also a reflection of man's uncritical nature that intellectuals, revulsed by what they saw, focused their attention on alternative systems to the near-total exclusion of any critical analysis of why the crash had occurred. Only a handful of mavericks, including professors Irving Fisher and Maynard Keynes, correctly identified money as the root of the evil.

Long before their ideas had become popular in the academic world, however, the onset of World War II and mobilization expenditures sparked an expansion in the money stock sufficient to reflate the economy and bring it to a state of optimum production. How ironic that it took the greater catastrophe of war to reverse the disaster of depression and rescue the financial independence of millions of people.

There were widespread fears that the postwar period would lead to another crash. But just as a recession appeared imminent, the outbreak of the Korean war resulted in an infusion of new money hot off the printing presses. Meanwhile, Keynes's views had penetrated the academy. The resulting consensus and subsequent application of the principles of demand management led to a golden era of capitalism and the unprecedented prosperity of the working man.

Instead of vindicating the zero-sum mentality, the glorious '50s and early '60s proved the opposite. When business is booming, workers and industry prosper simultaneously. Good profits lead to capital expansion, which increases productivity sufficiently to permit a higher payout in real wages. A smoothly operating economy benefits capital and labor alike.

The mutual benefits of these halcyon years were so obvious that Marx was relegated to a back shelf. Universities taught his theory more under the category of general knowledge than as any practical substitute for the status quo. At the same time the totalitarian aspects of socialist experiments created doubts about the ultimate practicability of Utopian dreams.

Just about the time that capitalism appeared to have won its place in heaven, and people like me were saying that we had learned so much that we would never again do anything half as stupid as we had in permitting the great depression to occur, the scene began to change. In the 1970s we suffered high inflation and high unemployment simultaneously in defiance of orthodoxy. "Bafflegab" displaced analysis in diagnosing the new disease. The result was symptom-treating through the harsh application of monetary restriction in a blood-letting cure much worse than the disease.

The systematic application of monetarist theory that began in the mid-'70s retarded economic growth and ultimately caused another great business contraction, which hit the disaster level in 1982—the worst over-all performance since the great depression. It was serious enough to raise unemployment to the 10-million-plus mark in the United States, above 30 million in the Western industrialized world, and to bring the international monetary system precariously close to the brink of collapse.

The human distress caused by this sadistic policy has raised old fears about the viability of the system itself. Ancient doubts have been excavated from the recesses of the mind. And for the first time in decades people are wondering if the good times are gone forever. Francis Blanchard, head of the International Labor Organization, predicts that unemployment is likely to remain a major world problem for the next twenty years—not just in the overpopulated Third World, but in the industrialized world as well.

This bleak outlook triggered the response from the Bishops, who were "increasingly concerned about the scourge of unemployment that plagues our society to-day and the corresponding struggles of workers. . . ." Their paper cast doubt on the viability of capitalism and contained unmistakable political and ideological overtones.

The Most Reverend Edward Scott, Anglican Primate of Canada and Moderator of the World Council of Churches, may have been somewhat more even-handed in his welcoming address to that body's Vancouver assembly in July 1983. He claimed that communism and capitalism are both in retreat, having failed to "provide unity, direction, standards and courage to their respective communities." "An era is ending," proclaimed the Primate.

Such dire predictions fan ideological flames as old protagonists increase their efforts to hold or gain ground. Inevitably, the propaganda war and the cold war are inextricably linked, and it is profoundly distressing to see some of our political and military leaders betting most of their chips on a few missiles.

This is the Maginot Line mentality. In the final analysis a few more or less missiles is unlikely to tip any balance—even the balance of terror. While attention is focused on this first and visible line of defense, the battle is already being waged behind the lines. The real enemy is the vacuum of positive ideas that is undermining the soft underbelly of democracy.

I am not saying that the West can neglect the credibility of its deterrent, but rather that maintained, additional overkill is both redundant and wasteful. The most that a deterrent can do is to buy time to revitalize our system and make it impervious to rational intellectual attack. That is freedom's only hope because the war will ultimately be won or lost in the hearts and minds of men, and it is on this front that we have become most vulnerable.

It is as incredible as it is ironic that the West, which possesses the vast range of scientific and technical skills required to put men safely on the moon, has been unable to operate its economies with the same workmanlike efficiency. I don't wish to be unduly critical, but perhaps the difference is in the psyche of engineers and economists. The former normally start with a solid foundation and use that base to build complex structures to dizzying heights. The latter, in my experience, are prone to start with the ether and then work backward in the hope that an undiscovered foundation exists when ground zero is reached.

The rhythm of business cycles is a case in point. Tens of thousands of man-hours have been consumed looking for a mathematical formula that will explain the past and act as a guide for the future—this despite the fact that even a cursory examination of cycles reveals the money supply connection.

It has been changes in the rate of monetary expansion due to the happenstance discovery of new gold fields, or the ratio of imports to exports, and more recently the whims of central bankers or the proximity of elections that have determined cyclic wavelengths. These dubious factors are just as amenable to crystal balls as they are to any elusive equations, so the unrelenting search for the latter only makes a relatively simple problem seem complex.

On the positive side, it is now generally agreed that prewar cycles were the offspring of erratic demand. But it is not yet generally agreed that the inflation that began to canter in the late '60s and then to gallop by the mid-'70s was primarily wage-related and that the monetary accommodation that paced it was dictated by the political necessity of maintaining reasonable levels of employment.

Consequently, when persistent double-digit inflation became bothersome, the classic approach of squeezing the money supply, wrapped in its new monetarist cloak of respectability, was applied just as if the problem were too few goods. The result was a wrenching deflation that resulted in widespread bankruptcies, massive unemployment, and neuroses for bankers.

If recessions, including the most recent ones, were primarily due to the vagaries of monetary fluctuations, then Marx erred in his analysis. Cycles are endemic not to capitalism, but rather to the myopia of political and monetary pilots. They have not yet been programmed to fly straight and level.

It follows that the ideological split between left and right in politics, and later between the West and the Warsaw Pact, was based on a false premise. Simply stated, it is incorrect to assume that it is not possible to operate a liberal democracy and a private capital system with consistent full employment.

I believe that jobs for all who want to work is a realizable goal and that the left-right division is as phony as a $3 bill. Ask spokesmen for either group what they hope to accomplish and the replies are astonishingly similar. Both want better housing, better health care, cleaner air and water, stable prices, full employment, and a higher standard of living for all. The divergence is in the means to achieve these ends.

The right insists that government intervention is the fly in the ointment. If only there could be a general deregulation and government got out of the hair of business, then Adam

Smith's "invisible hand" would give direction to the market as it evolved to the betterment of all.

The left contends that the opposite is true. Private initiative has failed to provide adequate housing, health care for the poor, acceptable environmental standards, and the right to gainful employment—without which all other rights become a mockery. So government must pick up the slack, and if some freedoms have to be sacrificed on the altar of the common good, that is a small price to pay for economic security and a more basic equality.

Both extremes are built on quicksand. The kind of Simon Pure laissez faire envisaged by the right never did exist except in the imagaination. There has never been a total absence of government intervention, and there never will be. New cars, airplanes, drugs, and factories all have to meet certain standards of health and safety. The only question is where the line between conflicting benefits is drawn.

The left's view that governments can be all things to all people is equally naïve. The dead weight of too much bureaucracy can stifle initiative and curtail freedom of choice. Anyone who has enjoyed a shopping spree in Moscow will think twice before abdicating too many decisions to unfeeling, uncaring, and faceless individuals. Instead of solving people's problems, bloated bureaucracies have a way of making their solution near-impossible. Also, intervention can only go so far without leading to totalitarianism, which is a giant step backward for a very small gain.

Fortunately, the middle road leads to the best of both worlds. To the extent that government intervention is required, a higher quality would permit a lesser quantity. The myriad programs designed to treat symptoms could be reduced or eliminated if stagflation was permanently banned.

In this book I argue that there is no rational excuse for either inflation or unemployment and that their simultaneous occurrence does not defy analysis, as often alleged.

The kind of private capitalism associated with political democracy, where the maximum number of people make the bulk of decisions, can work not just acceptably but superbly! All we have to do is identify the reality of an evolving economic world, accept the result intellectually, and then have the will to implement appropriate policies.

There is no reason why the marriage of capitalism and liberal democracy cannot work indefinitely as successfully and productively as it did during the golden post – Korean war years. Then the system will no longer be under attack from within but, on the contrary, will provide a model genuinely worthy of emulation.

2

Demonic Stagflation

"Demonic" is an apt word to describe the mess we created. There is no disagreement with the Catholic Bishops on that point. When they say "we have also witnessed, first hand, the results of a troubled economy: personal tragedies, emotional strain, loss of human dignity, family breakdown, and even suicide," they do not exaggerate.[1] Stagflation results in a carnage of broken homes, marriages, lives, and hopes. It embodies certain aspects of war in the sense that it leaves casualties strewn across the landscape.

The inflation component is an insidious disease. Once it gets into the economic bloodstream, it spreads quickly and soon gets out of control. Like most viruses, however, it affects some individuals more than others. We are not equally endowed with antibodies. The strong and the robust are relatively immune, while the old and the weak are alarmingly vulnerable.

Anyone living on a fixed income is caught in inflation's vise. A retirement income or endowment that appeared quite adequate a decade ago may have shrunk in purchasing power to the point where it is grossly inadequate and requires a traumatic adjustment in living standards. Some pensioners I know have adjusted continually—first from steak to hamburger and then doing without meat and getting by on macaroni.

The working poor comprise another very large group wounded by inflation. Minimum wages have lagged behind the increase in cost of living. Consequently, workers at the bottom of the scale are fast becoming second-class citizens who can't really afford the basic necessities. Their $3 to $4 an hour wages are insufficient for food, clothing, and shelter, let alone essential repairs and other ordinary costs of living.

I was reminded of their plight a while ago when we had a small electrical problem at our house. We phoned an electrician who dropped by and left a bill for $30 just for telling us we had a problem—a fact that had come to our attention before the call was placed. Needless to say, the bad news for repairs came later, when I thought to myself, "Good heavens, how could anyone earning $3.50 an hour afford to pay for any electrician?" They can't.

That's one of the insidious aspects of inflation: its injustice. Not only does it cripple the buying power of people on fixed incomes and the working poor, who in many cases would "enjoy" a higher disposable income if they quit their jobs and went on welfare; it attacks other individuals with the random discrimination of a lottery draw. The lucky, who had paid off their mortgages or who had long-term loans at low interest rates before the crunch came, were in clover. But anyone who had to renew a mortgage or borrow large sums to finance a business at high interest rates was struck an unexpected blow.

Inflation redistributes income by taking real wealth from some individuals and depositing it to the benefit of others.

For example, anyone who was fortunate enough to have a long-term, low-interest mortgage before the inflation of the late '70s and early '80s got underway repaid the loan with dollars that would only buy a fraction as much as the dollars borrowed. So the lender was robbed. And not all lenders were rich corporations; some of them were the widows who have been forced to give up their hamburger.

The bottom line for inflation is morality. Unlike other forms of stealing, however, inflation is not illegal. And one of the reasons we have been so reluctant to come to grips with the issue is because the most powerful elements in society, the best educated, the upwardly mobile middle class, trade unionists, and public employees were the least affected. Governments, too, were among the guilty. Revenues, swollen by inflation, were used to create the illusion of a "free lunch." But in the end, when it appeared the whole legerdemain might get out of control and the monetary brakes were applied, even the strong were exposed to the ravages of combined inflation and economic stagnation.

Farmers have been high on stagflation's hit list. Third- and fourth-generation livestock producers have had to abandon their way of life when high interest rates and low meat prices forced them out of business. Farm bankruptcies soared from 125 in 1979 to 410 in 1982. The statistics show only the tip of the iceberg, however, because they don't include receiverships and voluntary abandonment. The suffering is much more widespread than the story the cold figures tell and afflicts farmers across Canada.

Homeowners have been equally hard hit. In November 1979, the federal minister in charge of housing, the Honorable Elmer MacKay, told a Toronto audience, "Canada Mortgage and Housing Corporation has acquired, largely through mortgage defaults, more than 31,000 units of housing across Canada and is acquiring more every day."[2] Thousands of additional units have been repossessed in the intervening years. More than 20,000 families were forced to vacate between January 1, 1981, and June 30, 1983. Lower interest rates are slowly stemming the tide, but the mass eviction of the late '70s and early '80s will go on record as unprecedented since the great depression.

The American experience has been similarly tragic. In Oregon, for example, the number of houses repossessed by the State Department of Veterans Affairs grew to an all-time high of 778 in April 1983. The department sold a record 114 repossessed houses during the month, but took in 159 new ones. "Reselling repossessed houses," reported the Salem *Statesman-Journal*, "is a relatively new problem for the DVA."[3] It is a problem that has become all too typical across the United States and Canada, where tens of thousands of families have been uprooted from their homes.

As Chrysler Chairman L.A. Iacocca pointed out, business, too, has been far from immune. More than 20,000 businesses failed in 1982. "That's the worst record since 1932—68 bankruptcies a day. The bad guys went broke two years ago. It's the good guys who are going under now. And all those businesses and all their employees are lost to the marketplace."[4]

Surprisingly, American business failures in the first four months of 1983 were 40 percent higher than for the same period in 1982. Bankruptcy expert Edward I. Altman of New York University attributed this "astounding" and "unprecedented" development to "the devastating nature of the recent recession and to the fact that a large number of companies were so weakened by losses and high interest rates that their survival was doomed even without a general revival in the economy."[5]

Canadian business has been affected similarly. There were 10,765 bankruptcies in 1982 compared with 2,958 in 1975, during an earlier recession. And although failures in the first four months of 1983 were fractionally higher than for the same period in 1982, by mid-year the worst was over. The casualties dropped from 787 in June to 629 in July and that toll was 24 percent lighter than for the same month a year earlier.[6]

In retrospect, one of the most depressing experiences of the period was to read the auction sale notices in the Toronto *Globe and Mail*. The list of liquidations might include a nursery, a sawmill, a machine shop, and a furniture factory. Always in my mind's eye I could see the hopes and aspirations of the owners going up in flames. Everything they had dreamed of and worked for over the years was gone, including their savings. Their future as well as that of their employees was suddenly as uncertain as the "fire-sale" prices the auctioneer's hammer would bring.

Even worse than the larceny of inflation, the chaos it causes in financial markets, and the business failures that flow from economic downturn is the curse of unemployment induced by monetary means. Far from being the cathartic that saves men's greedy economic souls, it is a denial of the right to work and contribute to society in exchange for a wage sufficient to maintain dignity and self-esteem. The consequences of prolonged massive unemployment are incalculable. They include tragic increases in the rates of crime, suicide, psychiatric problems, alcoholism, and child abuse. It's a long and depressing list.

Anne Cohn, a representative of the National Committee for the Prevention of Child Abuse, a U.S. group, told a committee of the Ontario Legislature that the economic recession and rising unemployment led to a dramatic increase in child abuse in 1982. Audrey Hunter, spokesperson for a Hamilton-based group called Parental Stress Services, told the committee that she noticed an increase in child abuse in Hamilton in the wake of large-scale layoffs in the city's steel industry.

In Canada more people are trying to beat tough times by taking a potentially profitable chance on smuggling drugs into the country. Staff Sergeant Fred Foster of the Royal Canadian Mounted Police drug squad said, "It's all due to lack of jobs. People want to make money, so they take a chance. They have nothing to start with, so they have nothing to lose." On October 14, 1982, Foster added, "Twenty-one people were arrested on Friday, Saturday and Sunday and charged with attempting to smuggle drugs into Toronto International Airport. And the busy season is just starting."[7]

The list of heartbreaking stories that I have read or that I know of personally would fill volumes. But one particularly poignant Associated Press report from Fort Myers, Florida, will suffice to illustrate the depths of despair.

The tragedy began when Miguel Ange Ocasio, twenty-eight, and his wife Luce, twenty-one, sold their sons Oscar, two, and Miguel, one, to two couples in the Fort Myers area in June 1982 because they had no money for rent or food. A relative of one of the purchasers notified police and charges were laid. Mr. Ocasio was sentenced to a year in jail and

Mrs. Ocasio given five years' probation when the couple pleaded no contest to child-selling.

Charges against the buyers were dismissed after they agreed to testify against the Ocasios, and the children were turned over to the state's Department of Health and Rehabilitative Services and placed in a foster home. While there, Oscar was reportedly scalded, and broke an arm. On March 1, 1983, he was brought to Lee Memorial Hospital with a severe head injury.

Leonard Liszewski, the Ocasios' family lawyer, reported that Oscar was pronounced dead on Monday morning, March 7, after doctors unhooked a respirator. The coroner said the boy had been "brain dead" since he was brought to the hospital.

The boy's father swallowed rat poison in a suicide attempt while on leave from jail to attend his son's funeral. "We've just got one tragedy after another," said Ocasio's lawyer. "Hopefully, this is the last one."[8]

Admittedly, this bizarre chain of events is an extreme case, but even one is too many! There are literally millions of lesser cases of heartache and soul-scarring. As the December 20, 1982, copy of *Business Week* reported, even the unnerving 10.8 percent unemployment recorded in November understates the havoc wreaked on the labor markets: "Unemployment touches far more households than the rate of any one month suggests. According to a Conference Board study, more than one out of every five workers has suffered at least one spell of unemployment in the past 12 months. And in contrast to past recessions, the duration of the current slump has prevented many of the unemployed—even if they manage to find work for a time—from staying on the job long enough to qualify for jobless benefits. Fewer than half of the unemployed are currently receiving unemployment insurance checks."[9]

In August 1983 Statistics Canada released a study indicating that the real "full-time" unemployment rate was at least 13.5 percent—about 1.6 million—significantly higher than the official 11.2 percent figure announced earlier in the month. "The calculation adds half of those who are involuntarily working at part-time jobs—that is, half of those who are taking part-time work only because they can't get full-time work—to the number of officially unemployed."[10] Either way, the total number unemployed is a disgrace.

The figures also fail to show the difficulty that young college graduates are having as they try to enter the work force. "This is unprecedented for young people for the entire post – World War II period," said Samuel M. Ehrenhalt, the regional commissioner of the U.S. Department of Labor's Bureau of Labor Statistics. "Unemployment will show you people who have been laid off," he said, "but it won't show you those who are discouraged from entering the labor force."[11]

Beth C. Brotman, a twenty-four-year-old student in her last year at the New York University Law School, sent more than a hundred letters to law firms and district attorney's offices and sat through thirty interviews without receiving any job offers. "There was a sense that in previous years things seemed to go so well for the whole class," she said. "I thought, 'Get into N.Y.U. and it's a piece of cake after that,' but it's not like that." Miss Brotman said that while she was not at the top of her class, she has a good academic record.[12]

I have heard precisely the same story from University of Toronto and Osgoode Hall law graduates. Many have been unable to find a firm with which to article and have been forced to seek other employment opportunities—for which, in most cases, they are vastly overqualified. It is small consolation that some of their friends with engineering degrees are driving taxis.

The future appears equally bleak for thousands of unemployed workers whose jobs may be filled by robots. In a front page story entitled "Few on Layoffs May be Rehired," the May 16, 1983 edition of *The New York Times* reported that senior executives meeting at Hot Springs, Virginia, indicated that, as a result of automation and the need to be competitive, they would rehire few of the workers laid off during the recession no matter how strongly the economy recovers: "James H. Evans, chairman of the Union Pacific Corporation, the giant transportation concern, said 6,000 of his company's 44,000 employees were on layoff. 'Will they come back?' he asked. 'The answer is probably not'."[13] Members of the Business Council, comprising current and former chief executive officers of most of the country's biggest companies, said they "also see wrenching changes ahead for American workers—for young workers in particular."[14]

It is doubtful that Sherlock Holmes could unravel the mystery of why voters tolerate this kind of performance in a democracy. In Britain, for example, when 85 percent of the 3 million jobless left school at or before age sixteen, 74 percent think government training schemes don't help, 54 percent have not even had one job interview, and 71 percent are beginning to wonder if they'll ever get a job, why do only 25 percent blame Mrs. Thatcher?[15] *The Economist* obviously finds the answer inexplicable and observes that "the failure of the jobless to be cross with government means that politicians will probably continue with unemployment-creating policies which sensible people ought to be cross about."[16]

The Economist sounds a warning to smug politicians of all persuasions, which applies with equal force on both sides of the Atlantic. "Those with historical memories should be forewarned. . . . Politically, working-class Britons also swung apathetically conservative at the beginning of the slump of the 1930s, which so enraged the next lot of Oxbridge undergraduates coming along that the intellectuals among them began to worship Stalin while he was in his bloodbath. A heartless right wing often leads within a decade to a silly left fed from the universities down. The fan clubs least needed for the late 1980s are 'sophomores for Mr. Andropov', who is internationally more menacing than Stalin."[17]

Politicians who twitch at the thought that "the devil made 'em do it" might begin their penance by reviewing the historical process that led us into the present mess.

NOTES

1 *Ethical Reflections on the Economic Crisis*. Episcopal Commission for Social Affairs, Canadian Conference of Catholic Bishops, Concacan Inc., 1983.
2 In a speech to the Property Forum, Toronto, November 7, 1979.
3 *Statesman-Journal*, Salem, Oregon, May 5, 1983, p. 1C.
4 L.A. Iacocca, Chairman of the Board, Chrysler Corporation, at the Conference Board in New York, N.Y., February 17, 1983, p. 14.
5 *Business Week*, June 13, 1983, p. 20.
6 Source: Federal Department of Consumer and Corporate Affairs.
7 *Toronto Star*, October 14, 1982.
8 *Globe and Mail*, Toronto, March 9, 1983, p. 2.
9 *Business Week*, December 20, 1982, p. 18.
10 *Globe and Mail*, Toronto, August 17, 1983, p. 1.
11 *New York Times*, March 20, 1983, p. 1.
12 *Ibid.*, pp. 1, 20.
13 *New York Times*, March 16, 1983, p. 1
14 *Ibid.*
15 *The Economist*, December 4, 1982, p. 11.
16 *Ibid.*
17 *Ibid.*

3

A Brief Résumé

The reason that capitalism has behaved so erratically and that we are in such a mess today is that the system just grew like Topsy. It wasn't planned because no one knew in advance how it would evolve. And most of the refinements that we have worked out in retrospect have only occurred following much hardship and when crisis demanded that action be taken.

The rule that describes the phenomenon is one of general application. Technology overtakes the status quo, but it may be decades or centuries later before the consequent institutional changes occur. For example, scientific advances in agriculture and medicine have reduced mortality rates dramatically, yet it took decades for some of the churches to adjust their thinking on the question of birth control. It was easier for them to cling to the old notion that high birth rates are essential to propagate the human race and exercise dominion over the earth.

Economics falls into that same category. The advent of the Industrial Revolution brought a change of unprecedented magnitude. Augmenting human labor with steam and then other forms of inanimate energy resulted in the output of goods on a scale hitherto unknown. Sometimes there was enough money to buy this wealth of new merchandise and sometimes there was not. It never occurred to anyone that a quantum jump in output would require an equally innovative system of distribution. The old monetary system wasn't flexible enough to cope.

For millennia, commerce has been conducted largely through either the barter system or the use of metal coins, usually of copper, silver, or gold. These modes of exchange proved inadequate to an industrial age and were supplemented by a banking system that also grew like Topsy. Private banks issued their own gold and silver certificates, which were used as currency. And as long as the system was unregulated, they were likely to issue an excess of certificates, which resulted in inflation when too much money was chasing a limited quantity of goods. Later, when the issue of notes was regulated and tied systematically to the reserves of gold and silver bullion held in bank vaults, the quantity of money alternated between too much and too little, depending on whether gold was being shipped into or out of the country, and on the happenstance discovery of new sources of the precious metal. The fact that the supply of money was not directly related to the supply of goods, but rather to extraneous factors, created chaos within the system.

When there was an excess of money, business expanded rapidly and prices rose to skim off the surplus. But when the availability of money was too meager to purchase all the goods available, business slowed down and unemployment plagued the economy, taking its human toll. This periodic shortage of purchasing power was obvious to laymen. Many, repelled by the consequences, tried to find a path through the

monetary jungle. Unfortunately, because they were not pro-
fessionally trained and because many of their solutions were
half-baked, they were generally regarded as "cranks."

Economists, meanwhile, had their heads buried com-
fortably in the sand, and refused to admit that any shortage
of purchasing power existed. They clung tenaciously to the
spirit of the early nineteenth-century French economist Jean
Baptiste Say's law, which states that since the production of
any article creates an equal demand for some other article,
total supply must equal total demand and, consequently,
there could be no such thing as general overproduction.

There were, of course, some sparkling exceptions. Irving
Fisher, a professor of economics at Yale in the early twentieth
century, specialized in monetary theory with the objective of
moderating both booms and depressions.

He discerned, correctly, that rising prices had been the
result of too much money, falling prices of too little. Like
everyone else, he was concerned about roaring inflation,
which creates panic and makes money increasingly worthless;
but he went further and considered all cycles undesirable.
Moderate fluctuations in the price level should be avoided
since rising prices encourage everyone to buy in the hope of
gaining speculative profits, while falling prices lead everybody to sell or refrain from buying. These mass waves of
buying and selling only intensify the severity of business
cycles and changes in employment.

But how much money is enough? Fisher thought the
practical test was what happens to prices. Rising prices
should lead to restriction of the money supply, falling prices
to its expansion. This is the essence of the quantity theory of
money, which in its simplest form states that in order to

maintain stable prices, the money supply should be increased or decreased in direct proportion to the output of goods and services.

Despite the logic of Fisher's analysis, it was not until John Maynard Keynes rejected the conventional wisdom that the "professionals" began to question the classical assumptions. The orthodoxy of the British economist David Ricardo (1772 – 1823) had not been successfully challenged for more than a century since Malthus. The latter had been aware of the shortage of purchasing power by simply observing the obvious. Because he was unable to explain in detail how this shortage arose, however, he was unable to dent the classical fortress.

Keynes realized instinctively that a periodic shortage of purchasing power, or "aggregate demand," was a serious problem and couldn't understand why it had been dismissed so summarily by his peers. He argued that recessions were caused, not by increased demand for money and rising interest rates, but more often from a sudden collapse in investment spending due to businessmen's view of future prospects.[1]

What Keynes didn't explain as clearly as he might have is that the periodic slump in business investment was a product of insufficient demand in the economy at large. Businessmen are not normally total fools, so when they can't sell all the goods they have for sale, they are naturally cautious about borrowing money to buy machinery to increase an already excess capacity.

A logical question arises as to why businessmen, faced with surplus goods, didn't cut prices to increase sales. In some cases they did. But often they didn't because to do so they had to reduce costs in order to make a profit. And one of the costs that wasn't easy to reduce was labor.

The British radical recognized the difficulty in this area. He observed a stiff resistance to wage decreases even under conditions of heavy unemployment. In Keynes's view, money wages would be inflexible downward—even without the pressures of unions and minimum-wage laws that tend to limit competition in the labor market.[2]

This is just common sense, or elementary psychology if you prefer. To maintain full employment with rising output and a fixed money supply, all prices, including wages, would have to adjust continually downward. What graduate student starting out with a salary of $15,000 would relish being told that with hard work he could expect a 2 to 3 percent annual reduction in pay and that his income at retirement would be a fraction of his initial stipend?

It doesn't matter that the lower salary would buy more in real terms. Being human, and a mite acquisitive by nature, we prefer the alternative system of increasing wages from year to year to reflect the increases in our productivity. But that requires a constant increase in the money stock commensurate with the increased volume of goods and services. Otherwise there wouldn't be enough money to go around.

Although Keynes did not directly challenge the inevitability of business cycles in his general theory, he did propose that governments act as a balance wheel to mitigate their effects. When business is slack and unemployment is high they should indulge in deficit financing of public works to stimulate the economy. Then, should the economy become overheated, taxes should be raised and some of the debt retired.

It was the consensus that finally developed around Keynes's views that gave rise to the fifteen or so glorious years of expansion that followed the Korean war. Productivity was high. Wages increased, but only slightly more than productivity. The money supply was increased at a rate that cleared the market and made jobs available for just about anyone who wanted to work without overheating the economy and creating demand inflation. Theory and practice were very much in tune, and the result was an unprecedented abundance of material wealth.

About the time it appeared that the Keynesian honeymoon would go on forever, it was soured by the appearance of an unwelcome intruder. The simultaneous occurrence of high inflation and high unemployment was a development that had not been provided for in the textbooks, and economists soon lost their easy self-assurance. The famous Swedish economist Gunnar Myrdal was quick to coin the word "stagflation" to describe the new and disturbing phenomenon, but he confided in an interview that applying the tag was much easier than explaining the cause.

In looking for reasons it was obvious that there had been a substantial increase in the rate of expansion of the money supply. The data showed clearly that it was well ahead of the increase in real output and this was inflationary. What was less clear were the reasons for the rapid expansion. It was variously attributed to larger government deficits, the impact of rapidly rising oil prices, or the effects of the Vietnam war. Most American economists traced the inflation component to a demand shock created by that war and President Johnson's simultaneous introduction of new social programs. Taxes were not increased soon enough and the money stock was expanded to accommodate the deficit.

I will discuss some weaknesses in each of these arguments in the next chapter and then make the case that labor unit costs rising at unprecedented rates was the predominant contributor to the inflationary aspect of stagflation. Higher unemployment and lower productivity followed because in subsequent years the monetary authorities refused to print money fast enough to provide jobs for all at the new higher price levels.

It was the failure to identify the impact of wage increases wildly in excess of productivity that led economists off into the wilderness once again. Just as their predecessors failed to recognize the downward rigidity of wages and prices, contemporary practitioners underestimated the incredible upward momentum of the wage-price spiral fueled by the monopoly power of big trade unions and accommodated by the market power of their equally big employers. These giants set the standards toward which the whole economy was attracted as if toward a powerful magnet.

Monetarists are the latest reincarnation of conservative orthodoxy. They live under the spell of Fisher's monetary equation, which was perfectly valid in his day, when prices were determined largely by the quantity of money. If Fisher were alive today he would realize that due to the "cartelization" of labor and business, as some of my American friends call it, the demand for money can be influenced by rising costs. And that is precisely what happened in the real world of political economy as the money stock was increased to accommodate a reasonable level of employment at ever-higher unit costs and prices.

Seemingly oblivious to the connection between cause and effect, monetarists have insisted on treating the effects of cartelization by monetary means. Although they have succeeded in taking the steam out of the wage-price spiral, there is no guarantee that the change is permanent. In the meantime, the sadistic monetarist approach to economics has played havoc with output and employment, leaving one unholy mess in its wake.

NOTES

1 J.M. KEYNES, *The General Theory of Employment, Interest and Money* (London: Macmillan & Co. Ltd.; New York: St. Martin's Press, Inc., 1960).
2 *Ibid.*

4

False and Incomplete Diagnoses

If stagflation is a synthesis of inflation and unemployment, it is important to examine each element individually for clues to the chemistry of their coexistence. In this connection the accelerating inflation of the late '60s and early '70s appears to have been the precursor of high unemployment in the late '70s and early '80s. So we will follow the calendar and begin with inflation.

As with malignancy, argument rages as to the origin, type, and possible cures of contemporary inflation. Is it classic "demand" inflation? Some variety of "cost-push" inflation? Or some combination of these two—a situation in which some prices rise in response to excess demand and others as a result of higher costs?

In a 1973 article entitled "Prescribing Remedies for Inflation," the late Vincent Bladen, economics professor at the University of Toronto, suggested that there are five basic causes. In addition to monetary inflation, he mentioned government borrowing to finance wars or social programs, business expansion in excess of available savings, the cost-push of rising wages and prices, and finally a world food shortage. If his article had been written a year later, following the dramatic increase in oil prices, no doubt he would have included that as a sixth variety.

Bladen compared the various "causes" of inflation to fever in the human body: "Just as in medicine, it is essential to identify the specific organisms causing the trouble before prescribing the antibiotic known to be effective in controlling that specific organism, so in political economy, it is essential to identify the specific variety of inflation, the specific cause of a particular inflation, before prescribing a remedy."[1]

It does seem sensible to identify the nature of an illness before prescribing a cure. Yet one should not be misled by the medical analogy. Inflation is inflation whether the money supply is increased to pay for wars, to finance government deficits, or to maintain a reasonable level of employment in the face of rising costs. It is only for simplicity of analysis that I am dividing it into its two widely recognized categories: *demand inflation*, defined as too much money chasing too few goods, and *cost-push inflation*, in which costs push or chase prices (depending on which you think comes first, the chicken or the egg) to ever-higher heights in a never-ending spiral.

THE VIETNAM WAR

Many economists insist that all inflation, including cost-push, has its genesis in excess demand. The extent to which this is true is open to question. The record suggests that their conclusion may be more intuitive than empirical.

In any event, most U.S. economists trace the origin of the unacceptable inflation of the '70s and early '80s to a surplus of purchasing power generated by the Vietnam war. For example, it is Robert Lekachman's view that President Johnson's escalation of the war drained manpower from civilian output, while "defense-generated incomes simply added themselves to other incomes in the competition for civilian goods."[2] Congress and the White House did not drain off the excess demand through higher taxes until 1968. Meanwhile unions bargained, successfully, to compensate for past inflation and to hedge against future inflation.

This opinion was endorsed by President Carter's Council of Economic Advisers, who wrote, "It was excess aggregate demand during the Vietnam war that drove up the underlying rate of inflation from 1 per cent to 4 or 5 per cent by the end of the 1960s."[3] Years after the fact, in his 1983 report, Bank of Canada Governor Gerald Bouey climbed on that same bandwagon.

The theory was enshrined in the ninth edition of Paul Samuelson's textbook, *Economics*, the Bible of budding economists. Samuelson noted that "low unemployment rates—as in the post 1965 boom, when the average dropped below 4 per cent—are associated with a quickening of price inflation."[4]

This widely accepted view leaves some very large questions unanswered. Neither Samuelson nor Lekachman has taken the trouble to explain why even lower unemployment rates in 1952 and 1953—the lowest in more than a quarter-century—were achieved without any comparable impact on prices. In fact, the inflation curve at that time was downward.

In addition, the Vietnam theory does not explain what happened outside the United States. If Governor Bouey is

correct when he says "demand pressures showed up first in
the United States, largely associated with the Vietnam war,
and later elsewhere,"[5] how does he account for the fact that
wages and prices began their steep ascent in Canada and the
United Kingdom a year or so before they did in the United
States?[6] Neither country was significantly affected by American involvement in Southeast Asia; therefore to conform with
the conventional wisdom their surge in prices should have
followed rather than preceded the one in America.

DEMAND SHOCKS

The "it started with Vietnam" school has been extended
into a general theory in an attempt to explain the ratchetlike
escalation of prices over the fifteen-year period from 1965 to
1980. The Vietnam war is now cited as just the first of three
major events that caused the rate of inflation to surge
upward.

In his final Economic Report to Congress, Jimmy Carter
said the second, which came in the early 1970s, "was associated with the first massive oil-price increase, a worldwide
crop shortage which drove up food prices, and an economy
which again became somewhat overheated in 1972 and
1973. The third inflationary episode came in 1979 and 1980.
It was principally triggered by another massive oil-price
increase, but part of the rise in inflation may also have been
due to overall demand in the economy pressing on available
supply."[7]

All well and good. No one denies that each of the three
shock waves affected prices. But Carter went on to explain

that "late in each of the three inflationary episodes monetary and fiscal restraints were applied, and at the end of each a recession took place, with rising unemployment and idle capacity."[8] On the basis of classical theory, as well as of Newton's law of gravitation, prices should then have come down to the previous levels. They had adjusted on innumerable occasions in earlier decades, so why not now?

President Carter's hindsight was dead on when he observed: "A set of inflationary causes raises the rate of inflation; when the initiating factors disappear, inflation does not recede to its starting position despite the occurrence of recession; the wage-price spiral then tends to perpetuate itself at a new and higher level. . . . It is this downward insensitivity of inflation in the face of economic slack that has given the last 15 years their inflationary bias."[9] What he didn't explain is where the "downward insensitivity" came from.

In reviewing Presidents' reports, and those of their economic advisers, I have found periodic temporary shortages of various goods that would explain why an increase in price would occur. I have been unable to unearth examples, with the possible exception of energy, where the shortage was sufficiently prolonged to sustain a permanent price rise. Consequently, I find the demand shock theory, in isolation, untenable.

In rejecting the Vietnam and demand-shock theses, I wish to underline that I am not speaking of other days and other times. The demand inflation generated as an aftermath of war is well documented.[10] Today, however, this is not a relevant factor. World War II and Korea are distant memories, and any effects from the Vietnam war, which were probably overstated, have long since dissipated.

GOVERNMENT DEFICITS

Another frequently cited scapegoat for inflation is government deficits. A group of prominent Canadian economists, in a letter to the Prime Minister in December 1975, stated that of three domestic causes of inflation, "first is the growth in government deficits: federal, provincial and municipal."[11] The same opinion is held by many American businessmen and economists. In "Causes and Effects of Inflation," C. Lowell Harriss states that "federal deficits are widely assumed to be a source, perhaps the chief source, of inflation."[12]

This widespread belief is milked to advantage by political parties in opposition. The Tories used the issue to advantage in the 1979 Canadian federal election and again since their subsequent defeat in 1980. Ronald Reagan made it an article of faith in rousing the righteous indignation of the American moral majority—though now the shoe is on the other foot. Still, for conservatives everywhere the "evil" of big budgetary deficits is accepted as faithfully as holy writ.

Harriss went on to say: "Such a conclusion is not necessarily accurate. The Federal Reserve faces no legal or economic compulsion to provide the banking system with extra reserves so that banks can create money (deposits) to buy the additions to federal debt. The Treasury may go into the capital markets, and by borrowing there, reduce the amounts available for utilities, housing, manufacturing, and other borrowers."[13]

President Reagan's Council of Economic Advisers tacitly acknowledged this distinction in their 1982 report. "The impact of a specific deficit will vary, however, depending on the conditions that lead to it. For example, during a recession—as now exists—the borrowing requirements of business and consumers tend to be relatively small. At such a time a given deficit can be financed with less pressure on interest rates than during a period of growth, when business and consumer demands for credit are increasing. That is why it is important for the government to reduce the budget deficit in fiscal 1983 and beyond, a period of anticipated rapid economic growth when private investment demands are expected to rise substantially."[14]

Ironically, the monetarist approach to inflation fighting is incompatible with fiscal conservatism. "During the last year, better-than-expected progress on inflation has reduced taxable income, slowing the growth of revenues below earlier projections. The recession has temporarily slowed the growth of the tax base while increasing outlays for employment-related programs."[15] So to the extent that deficits are really inflationary, much of what has been gained on the monetary swing has been lost on the fiscal roundabout.

There are economists who doubt that deficits have been a major contributor to inflation. In Canada the conventional wisdom was effectively challenged by Robert B. Crozier when he was senior economist for the Conference Board of Canada. In a 1976 study entitled *Deficit Financing and Inflation: Facts and Fictions*,[16] Crozier showed that, in Canada, deficit financing had been a negligible factor contributing to inflation. What had been more important was the increasing proportion of total output spent by governments. The high taxes required to finance these expenditures added considerably to unit costs both directly, as a significant element in prices, and indirectly, by increasing labor demands for higher wages. Thus government expenditures have been an important contributor to cost-push (or tax-push, as some people like to call it) inflation.

Jimmy Carter's advisers entered a note of caution on the same subject: "If government budget deficits are the cause of inflation, it should make no difference whether the deficit occurs at the Federal, State or local level. . . . The combined budgets of Federal, State and local governments have either showed a surplus or a really small deficit during the past two decades, except during recessions and for two years when Federal spending on the Vietnam war was at its peak.

"This notion that budget deficits are the chief cause of inflation also founders on a comparison of budget deficits and inflation among different countries. Japan and Germany in recent years have had much better success in combating inflation than the United States. Yet their budget deficits, especially those of Japan, have been much higher relative to the size of their economies than has been the case in the United States."[17]

I have long been convinced that budget deficits are neither the sole nor principal cause of contemporary inflation in Western industrialized economies. There is much evidence to the contrary. That said, it doesn't follow that the size of the deficit is unimportant. It depends, as a politician might say, on the circumstances.

Reagan's Council of Economic Advisers made the categorical assertion that "it is now generally agreed that continued excessive growth in the money supply will cause sustained inflation. Thus, deficits financed by money creation will have persistent inflationary consequences."[18]

The second half of the statement is true only in the context of the preamble where the operative word is "excessive." If the growth in the money supply is excessive there will be inflation with or without deficits. If the expansion of the money stock is not excessive the impact of a deficit will depend, as Lowell Harriss suggested, on where the money to make up the shortfall comes from. One has to look at the total expansion in the money supply, and the use to which it is put, in order to evaluate the impact of deficit financing.

If a government increases its deficit to buy another car for the police, the net effect would be the same as if an individual borrowed the same amount of money to acquire a vehicle for his own private use. That said, in both cases the impact on the economy would depend on whether the automobile industry was already operating at capacity.

I accept Harriss' conclusion: "If the economy has much unutilized productive capacity, money creation may finance benefits from government spending without loss of either output or price level increases."[19] If, on the other hand, the capacity of the economy is fully utilized, printing more money will be inflationary regardless of whether the extra cash is used for public or private purposes.

THE ENERGY CRISIS

Another diagnosis attributes inflation to the effects of the rapid escalation of oil prices. The world price of oil soared from $3 to $11.65 a barrel between October 1, 1973, and January 1, 1974, resulting in American consumer price increases of 75.5 percent for gasoline and motor oil, 247.5 percent for fuel oil and coal, and 40.6 percent for gas and electricity.[20]

Former Treasury Secretary William E. Simon told a Senate Subcommittee on September 8, 1974, that "the quadrupling of oil prices over the past year, when its effects are fully felt, will have contributed in the range of 5 to 8 percentage points in our wholesale price index." He added that this was about half the increase in the index for the year ending in mid-1974.[21] Later statistics put the effects of the oil-price rise in better perspective. Joel Popkin, a staff member of the President's Council of Economic Advisers, said that energy prices to consumers increased 33.5 percent in the year after the cost of imported oil shot upward, while consumer prices as a whole jumped 11.2 percent. Popkin estimated that energy was responsible for just under one-fifth of the increase in the cost of living.[22]

In Canada, where the increase in oil prices has been controlled, the energy component of inflation has been even less. Conference Board of Canada analysts estimate that, on average, energy contributed about one-tenth of the increase in the Consumer Price Index for the 1975 – 81 period.

Still, politicians used the actions of the oil cartel as an excuse for the inflation they didn't understand and seemed powerless to control. In his January 1980 Report to Congress, President Carter cited oil prices as "the major reason for the worldwide speedup in inflation during 1979 and the dimming of growth prospects for 1980."[23]

By 1982 the worm had turned. Increased output by non-OPEC countries, including Britain, Norway, and Mexico, combined with slack demand due to conservation measures and the world-wide recession, created an oil glut. Prices turned soft and by the end of the year were exerting downward pressure on the Consumer Price Index.[24]

At an extended meeting in March 1983 the OPEC ministers finally came to grips with the new reality and agreed to an official reduction of $5 a barrel to bring their prices in line with the new world price. They also agreed to restrict production simultaneously. No one knows how long this uneasy accord will last. But it is clear that the once all-powerful cartel will be hard pressed to maintain some semblance of order in the market until demand overtakes supply once more.

Reflecting on the impact of oil prices in the 1970s, one might ask why some countries were so much more successful than others. West Germany and Switzerland both import a higher proportion of their oil needs than do Canada and the United States. It would follow that if oil was the major disrupting factor in economic performance, their records should have been poorer than ours. In fact, they were much better.

For a time when the Oil Producing and Exporting Countries had their act together the whole world shook, yet statistics show that the cartel was given far too much blame for a problem that has been, for the most part, domestic in origin.

THE GOLD STANDARD

Another diagnosis that is often cited as the root cause of inflation is the fact that our currencies are not convertible into gold. Many writers, including Henry Hazlitt, former financial writer and columnist for *The New York Times*, insist that currencies can be stable only if they are gold-backed. It is a virulent mythology.

Even Winston Churchill was mesmerized by the old golden order. He tried putting England back on the gold standard in the mid-1920s when he was Chancellor of the

Exchequer. Stressing the importance of simultaneous action by other countries, he pictured the advantages in this metaphor: "That standard [the gold standard] may of course vary from time to time, but the position of all countries related to it will vary together like ships in a harbour whose gangways are joined and who rise and fall with the tide."[25] Churchill based his case on the opinions of "experts" and, in particular, on the Report of the Committee on the Currency and Bank of England Note Issue. The general advantages of the gold standard were not stated by the report, but were taken for granted as self-evident.

The passing years proved that Churchill's metaphor was intuitive but in a perverse sense: "With the ebb tide of liquidity at the outset of the depression, the 'ships of the harbour' sank into the mud and lay there, immobile, until 1939 when the rising tide of mobilization expenditure raised the rusty hulls."[26] In fact, the return of the gold standard in the United Kingdom had just caused an overvalued pound, which only intensified the problem of industrial expansion and restricted international trade.

Two problems are endemic to a gold-backed currency. First, the rate of discovery and availability of gold seldom corresponds with the natural growth rate of an economy. Historically, there has usually been either too much or too little. One of the worst inflations Europe has known followed Columbus's success in crossing the Atlantic. "Discovery and conquest set in motion a vast flow of precious metal from America to Europe, and the result was a huge rise in prices— an inflation occasioned by an increase in the supply of the hardest of hard money.[27]

Second, when international transactions were settled in

gold, difficulties arose. When excess imports were paid for by sending bullion out of the country, the monetary base was contracted, and recession followed. When the opposite occurred and an export surplus brought gold flowing into the country, the monetary base was expanded, resulting in inflation. This cycle was never consistent with operating a domestic economy in the interests of its citizens.

A clear distinction should be made between the usefulness of gold as an adjunct to international trade and its relevance to the growth and stability of a domestic economy. Gold may have a place in a new international monetary order, as there may be "sellers" who prefer payment in gold (a commodity), or a new gold-backed international currency, rather than any single national currency or composite paper money. Gold's intrinsic value and relative scarcity have given it a long history as one of the items for which people will trade their goods and services.

At the same time, gold is not an essential ingredient to a strong, stable domestic economy. If all the gold in the United States and Canada were to disappear mysteriously overnight, the capacity of our economies would be unaffected except for rare instances, such as the manufacture of jewelry, where the yellow metal is used as a raw material. Domestic prices might continue to rise, but for reasons other than the presence or absence of gold.

PASSING THE BUCK

Finally, when all else fails and economists still feel uneasy about their analyses of contemporary inflation, they take refuge in the popular notion that it is an international problem largely beyond the competence of individual nation states. They argue that the world economy has become so interdependent that it rises and falls like the tides. Any one country is like a cork on the surface, unable to influence its own movement.

Politicians, taking their cue from the experts, and not knowing what else to say, use the argument repeatedly. One of Prime Minister Trudeau's aides admitted candidly, "Until we get a better handle on it [inflation] we have to pass the buck." Consequently, to the extent a government appears powerless to curb prices, it says the problem is imported (in Canada from the United States and in the United States from OPEC). Journalists duly report the explanation, and the public, who have heard the story a thousand times, have swallowed the whale.

The theory is expounded in the Mundell-Laffer Hypothesis.[28] Rather than view the United States or any other economy as closed, with international relationships grafted on, these two economists insist that the only closed economy it makes sense to talk about is the world economy. One cannot understand the U.S. economy from an American perspective; it must be viewed from a global perspective.

Certainly no country is an island unto itself. A severe frost in the coffee plantations of Brazil affects the world-wide price of the aromatic bean. A similar freeze in Florida boosts the price of orange juice in both Canada and the United States. A major wheat shortage in the Soviet Union influences the market for grain in North America just as surely as does a crop failure at home. A sudden disappearance of the anchovy off the coast of South America creates unforeseen and far-reaching effects on soy-bean prices in the American Midwest.

It is also true that actions in the monetary field in one powerful jurisdiction affect the ability of other countries to pursue an independent course. As gyrations in the U.S. price of money, from the fall of 1979 to date, have landed on Canadian shores with force, Governor Bouey explained: "Movements of this magnitude in U.S. interest rates were bound to have substantial effects on interest rates in Canada or on the foreign exchange value of the Canadian dollar or on both."[29] Had Canadian interest rates not been raised in concert with those of our southern neighbor, ours would have been uncompetitive and capital would have flowed out of the country. So, reluctantly, or otherwise, Canada's central bank looks like a monkey on the Fed's back (the Federal Reserve Board is commonly known as the Fed).

As Mundell and Laffer point out, there is evidence that prices, including the price of money, tend to seek a world level. But it is also true that some countries have a much better record in matters of employment and price stability than others. Two countries with better-than-average performance are Switzerland and West Germany, both of them open economies, heavily involved in world trade and financial transactions. The Federal Republic of West Germany has managed its economy exceptionally well, at least until recently. The 1979 inflation rate of 5 percent was a matter of real concern to officials there, but it looked very appealing to those of us contending with double that level—especially when the unemployment rate in Germany at 3.8 percent was also much lower than in Canada (7.5 percent) and the United States (5.8 percent).[30] The Swiss performance topped even that of the Federal Republic.[31]

Equally puzzling, in the context of the Mundell-Laffer hypothesis, was the wide disparity between U.S. and Canadian rates of inflation when the U.S. rate dropped dramatically to 6 percent by the end of 1982 while the figure for Canada was still 10.8. There has to be some important factor beyond the contention that the tide is only slowly rolling across the 49th parallel. The explanation could lie in the disparity between industrial wage increases in the United States (4.6 percent) and Canada (11 percent) in 1982.

I admit that no country with an open economy can prevent changes of individual prices affected by world markets. But that doesn't explain or excuse a general rise in prices when the price of oil, lumber, or food goes up. In a free market, with a fixed money supply, some prices must fall when others go up. When people only have so much money to spend and they decide to spend more for one item, then they automatically must spend less on something else. Demand for the other item or items declines, and prices fall accordingly. Consequently, any country in control of its own currency should be able to maintain a constant average price level—at least in theory.

Gerald Bouey almost made that point in his 1980 report where he said: "I do not regard increases in the price of one commodity, relative to another, as a valid reason for a general acceleration of the rate of inflation, because in a less inflationary environment faster-than-average increases in some prices would tend to be offset by slower-than-average increases in others.[32]

If it isn't necessary for the rate of inflation to increase when one price goes up, as the Governor maintains, then by the same logic it should be possible to maintain stable prices.

When some prices go up, others should come down. That is how the system should work in a pure market economy. Still, the professionals trot out increases in one commodity as justification for a general price rise; they refuse to admit that we haven't had, don't have, and never will have a "pure" market economy. They just keep pretending that black and gray are white.

NOTES

1 "Prescribing Remedies for Inflation," *Globe and Mail*, Toronto, August 29, 1973.

2 ROBERT LEKACHMAN, *Inflation: The Permanent Problem of Boom and Bust* (New York: Vintage Books, 1973), p. 37.

3 Annual Report of the Council of Economic Advisers, Washington, D.C., January 1981, p. 39.

4 PAUL A. SAMUELSON, *Economics*, 9th ed. (New York: McGraw-Hill Book Co., 1973), p. 829.

5 Bank of Canada Annual Report, February 27, 1981, p. 16.

6 O.E.C.D. Main Economic Indicators, 1965 – 70.

7 Economic Report of the President, January 1981, pp. 7 – 8.

8 *Ibid.*, p. 8.

9 *Ibid.*

10 MILTON FRIEDMAN, *A Program for Monetary Stability* (New York: Fordham University Press, 1960).

11 The letter was written by John Crispo and Douglas Hartle of the University of Toronto and signed by all seventeen.

12 LOWELL HARRISS, "Causes and Effects of Inflation," in *Inflation: Long-Term Problems* (New York: The Academy of Political Science, 1975), p. 11.

13 *Ibid.*, pp. 11 – 12.

14 Annual Report of the Council of Economic Advisers, February 1982, pp. 95 – 96.

15 *Ibid.*, p. 95.

16 ROBERT B. CROZIER, *Deficit Financing and Inflation: Facts and Fictions*. The Conference Board in Canada, March 1976.

17 Economic Report of the President, January 1981, pp. 41 – 42.

18 Annual Report of the Council of Economic Advisers, February 1982, p. 99.

19 LOWELL HARRISS, "Causes and Effects of Inflation," *op. cit.*, pp. 11 – 12.

20 Congressional Quarterly, 1975, p. 14.

21 *Ibid.*

22 *Ibid.*

23 Economic Report of the President, January 1980, p. 3.

24 Annual Report of the Council of Economic Advisers, February 1983, p. 225.

25 U.K. *Parliamentary Debates*, Volume CI xxxiii, Col 55.

26 PAUL T. HELLYER, *Agenda: A Plan for Action* (Toronto: Prentice-Hall of Canada, 1971), p. 13.

27 JOHN KENNETH GALBRAITH, *Money: Whence it Came, Where it Went* (New York: Bantam Books Inc., 1980), p. 13.

28 ROBERT A. MUNDELL, Professor of Economics at Cambridge, and Arthur B. Laffer, then of the University of Chicago Graduate School of Business.

29 Bank of Canada 1980 Report, Ottawa, March 1981, p. 9.

30 O.E.C.D. Main Economic Indicators, January 1982.

31 Switzerland's 1979 rates of inflation and unemployment were 5.2 and 0.3 respectively.

32 Bank of Canada Report, Ottawa, March 1981, p. 11.

5

Monetarism: A Cure
Worse Than the Disease

If the cause of contemporary inflation is still somewhat
obscure, the generally accepted prescription for its cure produces side effects more dreadful than the disease. The unemployment factor in stagflation is the direct result of treating
inflation by monetary means.

In the more than thirty years since I entered political life
the standard medicine for rising prices has been "tight
money." There have been a couple of half-hearted attempts at
incomes policies, but these were the exceptions. The normal
response to inflation has been to cut back the rate of increase
in the money supply.

Unfortunately, the result has always been painful and the
benefit never permanent. Inevitably output slowed, unemployment rose, and small business had its credit noose tight-
ened. The inflation rate dipped temporarily as wage
increases, especially non-union wages, were curbed slightly
and business profits were squeezed. But as soon as the jobless
rate approached the political flash point, the money supply
was eased and the situation returned to "normal" except for
the residue of disrupted lives, bankrupt enterprises, and the
irretrievable loss of production.

That accounts for my dismay bordering on outrage when the same hurtful formula was applied yet again. It was comparable to a sick person going to a doctor and being given pills that made him worse rather than better. And not just once but repeatedly. For the patient to meekly accept a near-lethal dose in response to the worsening inflation of the mid-'70s defies explanation. The prescription was nothing short of a savage attack on the body politic.

MONETARISM

In the early days we just called it "tight money." But with the ascendancy of Milton Friedman and the Chicago school of economic evangelism, the old snake venom was given the new and more sophisticated label of "monetarism."

The theory is splendid, almost classic. Inflation is caused by printing money faster than the increase in the supply of goods. Consequently, one only needs to slow down the presses that print money until their speed corresponds to the output of goods and services. Then, Bingo, prices will be stable.

Unfortunately, the theory conveniently ignores all factors other than monetary. This isolation from reality is the line of demarcation between monetarists and non-monetarists—including those who accept the central role of money as an economic stabilizer.

As a practical theory, monetarism fails on two fundamental and related counts. First, it assumes a degree of market perfection that doesn't exist and blissfully ignores the cartelization of an important segment of the economy. Second, in the same vein, it treats labor as just another price to be determined by market forces, along with other prices.

This is somewhat astonishing for readers of *Free to Choose*. In it Milton Friedman chronicles the history of monetary mismanagement and the resulting recessions and depressions. Speaking of the catastrophic '30s he says: ". . . we now know, as a few knew then, that the depression was not produced by a failure of private enterprise, but rather by a failure of government in an area in which the government had from the first been assigned responsibility—'To coin money, regulate the Value thereof, and of foreign Coin', in the words of Section 8, Article 1, of the U.S. constitution."[1]

Much of the rest of his book is a lament for the myriad intrusions of government in the marketplace—many of them designed to provide direct or indirect relief from the periodic recessions. It is a litany of the evil consequences of all those systems, either of preference or of restraint, "that Adam Smith fought against, that were subsequently destroyed, but have since reappeared in the form of to-day's tariffs, governmentally fixed prices and wages, restrictions on entry into various occupations, and numerous other departures from his 'simple system of natural liberty'."[2]

Friedman obviously recognizes that the market for labor has been altered by legislation and regulation. In his discussion of how the labor market operates he says: "Here, too, interference by government, through minimum wages, for example, or by trade unions, through restricting entry, may distort the information transmitted or may prevent individuals from freely acting on that information."[3]

Quite so! But having observed and objected to the rigidities in the labor market due to government intervention,

Friedman proceeds to ignore the connection between wages and prices by denying the existence of cost-push inflation. This gap in his reasoning leads to the conclusion that he is at the same time 80 percent right and 100 percent wrong—a neat trick even for a learned professor.

The Friedman analysis of where capitalism went wrong and his conclusion that business cycles were caused by monetary excesses is exactly what I believe. His concern that governmental intervention has reached the point where it actually impedes the satisfaction of human needs strikes a sympathetic chord and is consistent with my experience in the business world. But his solution to the problem of contemporary inflation is one that ignores the rigidities he deplores. For him labor is just another price freely determined in the market.

This blind spot has been noted by many critics. In *Capitalism's Inflation and Unemployment Crisis*, Sidney Weintraub says "to interpret money wages as simply another price is to mistake flies for elephants." A general wage rise "comprises 55 per cent of gross business costs, close to 75 per cent of net costs and probably even more of variable costs."[4] In fact, money wages constitute the major factor in the economic equation; they far outshadow any other price.

In view of this, one should not underestimate the significance of Dr. Friedman's unsubstantiated contention that "wage increases in excess of increases in productivity are a result of inflation rather than a cause."[5] It is very difficult to prove.

The Organization for Economic Co-operation and Development (O.E.C.D.) *Main Economic Indicators* data show that wages have outstripped productivity in the United

States in all but four years since 1960. In Canada there have been two exceptions: 1962 and 1964.

In the early '60s, when wages in the United States rose at approximately the same rate as productivity, price increases were very modest—slightly more than 1 percent. Canadian price increases were roughly comparable even though wages outstripped productivity by a comfortable margin. Later in the decade, settlements substantially outpaced productivity in both countries and as a result prices rose more quickly.

Not only have wages moved up faster than productivity, they have outpaced prices in all but a handful of years—the primary exceptions being around the turn of the decade when real wages fell. Figures 1, 2, and 3 show clearly that, as far back as 1960, which predates stagflation, nominal wages rose faster than prices. Wages led and prices followed in Canada, the United States, and the United Kingdom and in each case wages are still ahead.

The same graphs also raise questions about the monetarists' claim that the money supply expanded first and wages followed. The money supply per member of the labor force, which is the only fair unit basis for comparison, grew more or less in parallel with prices but less quickly than wages. Admittedly, there is a correlation between the growth in the money supply and the consumer price index, as monetarists claim; but there is an equally close or even closer relationship between prices and labor unit costs, as we will see later on.

Monetarism assumes elasticity of wages. So to the extent that union power and collective bargaining impede flexibility, monetarism becomes an irrational theory. It is rational for unions to optimize the advantage of their bargaining power. In expecting them to do otherwise than act in their own perceived best interests, monetarism is itself irrational.

Figure 3
Index of Wages, Prices, and the Money Supply per Member of the Labor Force in the United Kingdom, 1960 – 1981

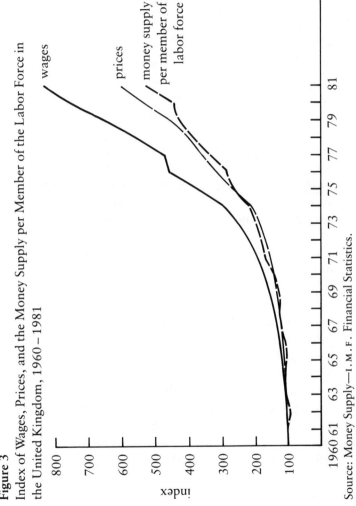

Source: Money Supply—I.M.F. Financial Statistics.

Wages and prices—O.E.C.D. Main Economic Indicators.

REAGANOMICS

The Reagan administration's approach to economics has been a unique blend of monetarism and "supply-side" economics. The relationship is set out in the report of the President's Council of Economic Advisers: "The speed with which the economy adjusts to the Administration policies will be largely determined by the extent to which individuals, at home and at work, believe the Administration will maintain, unchanged, its basic approach to personal and business taxation, Federal spending and regulation, and monetary policy. When public expectations fully adjust to this commitment, a necessary condition for both reduced inflation and higher growth will be fully established. In short, as this Report attempts to demonstrate, what some people have referred to as 'monetarism' and 'supply-side economics' should be seen as two sides of the same coin—compatible and necessary measures to both reduce inflation and increase economic growth."[6]

I frankly admit that the improvement on the inflation front has been somewhat greater than I anticipated. I have long recognized that U.S. labor is more pragmatic and less ideological than their Canadian and U.K. brothers, but I underestimated the extent to which American unions would recognize job security rather than wages as their number-one priority in 1982. There were other reasons why prices leveled out, including a turn-down in energy costs and a squeeze on profits. The combination of these factors brought the rate of inflation, temporarily, below the underlying rate.

If success in damping inflation exceeded my expectations, it is equally true that the cost was higher than predicted. "The progress that was made in reducing inflation, however, was accompanied by a painful slowdown of the economy. Beginning in July 1981, the nation suffered the second of two back to back recessions that brought the unemployment rate to 10.8 percent in December 1982. At that time, approximately 5 million more people were unemployed than in January 1980, when the first of the two recessions began."[7]

That frank assessment by the Council of Economic Advisers in their February 1983 report is a far cry from the optimistic hope of Jerry L. Jordan, a former member (1981) of Reagan's Council of Economic Advisers, who predicted that the job could be done "with only a mild recession that would cure itself as the Fed's policy of restraint began to be believed."[8]

In summary, the "monetarist" side of the government's coin produced dramatic though not necessarily permanent results on the inflation front. The "supply-side" failed miserably in achieving its goal of increased economic growth. On that score it was a case of one step forward and two steps backward.

SUPPLY-SIDE ECONOMICS

Ronald Reagan touched the heart of America with the rosy picture of economic prospects he painted during the 1980 election. All that the United States needed to do, he suggested, was abandon the Keynesian dogma that governments can stabilize the economy by judicious management of aggregate demand—as espoused by the Democrats—and return to that old-time religion of discouraging sloth and rewarding effort. It was a sermon upholding the classical free-market tradition of economics, and the majority of voters loved it.

Reagan's brand of supply-side economics assumed that rapid growth was possible under the right economic circumstances. His policy was founded on the theory, championed by a number of economists including Arthur B. Laffer,[9] that cutting taxes and allowing workers and investors to keep more of what they earn will increase both investment and work effort. "Growth will result from the freeing of the supply side rather than from the Keynesian management of demand."[10] And increased revenues from an expanding economy will offset any loss resulting from the lower tax rates.

Actually, the principles of supply-side economics are not new. They comprise old concepts in a slick new Hollywood package. In fact, certain aspects of it are just common sense and date back at least as far as 5 A.D. *The Economist* recounts the story: "When Octavian became Caesar Augustus, the imperial finances were in a shambles. The state was not able to raise enough from a mass of complex duties and taxes to pay for its military and civil follies. So, as Tacitus and St. Luke tell us, 'a decree went out from Caesar Augustus that all the world should be taxed.' That famous census, at the time of Christ's birth, took some years to bear fruit.

"Augustus was no Thatcherite or Reaganaut. He enjoyed subsidizing food, and huge public works, but his adviser, Maecenas, was an early believer in supply-side miracles. He urged the wholesale auction of state property and the lending out of the money raised at cheap interest rates so that agriculture and industry could flourish. Laffer-like, he argued that lower and simpler taxes could mean more revenue."[11]

Certainly the converse is true, as examples from my own experience will illustrate. The head nurse in an old folks' home in Toronto's Trinity riding stopped working Saturdays after she and her husband figured out how much of her income the government took and what was left. A CBC TV cameraman, without dependants, cut out overtime assignments for the same reason.

There are almost as many permutations as there are people. Quite a few tradesmen I know will fix windows or cement patios in the evening or on weekends—but only for cash. My tailor told me that several of his most skilled needleworkers moved their operations to their homes so that they could work on a cash basis. Some of them collected unemployment insurance illegally until their benefits ran out.

Quite a few of my friends who are in the top tax brackets used to spend as much time with their lawyers and accountants looking for loopholes to beat the system as they did producing new wealth until Finance Minister Allan MacEachen reduced the marginal rate in his 1981 budget. Consistent with theory, tax havens appear much less attractive now than they did when governments skimmed off two-thirds of the cream.

The hope of stimulating economic activity through tax cuts and other incentives is often exaggerated, however. Don Fullerton, of Princeton University, attempted to pinpoint where the United States is located on a Laffer-type curve for the Office of Tax Analysis of the Treasury Department. Fullerton concluded: "The U.S. economy is far from operating in the prohibitive range of the Laffer curve, where high tax rates would stifle so much work activity that total tax revenues would be hurt."[12]

There is also some doubt about the effectiveness of measures designed to stimulate capital investment in industry. A study of the implicit tax subsidies involved in the accelerated depreciation and investment credit policies implemented by eight industrial countries since 1973 failed to find any positive correlation between advantageous treatment and results. George F. Kopits of the International Monetary Fund discovered that the least advantageous systems are found in Japan and Germany—countries that have managed to maintain high rates of capital formation. *Business Week* concludes: "The unstated but obvious lesson of Kopits' analysis is that those nations that have kept a rein on inflation have apparently little need of such subsidies, while those that have resorted to subsidies have found them of little help as long as they were implemented in an inflationary environment."[13]

Supply-side measures will have little effect in stimulating growth as long as they are the obverse side of the monetarist coin. Productivity might be marginally enhanced with the use of new and better machinery. But at the end of the day who is going to spend scarce cash on new machinery when demand is slack and existing capacity lies idle? This was the point that Lord Keynes glossed over in his general theory. He attributed the periodic downturn in the business cycle to a shortage of capital investment. Had there been a lively market for goods, someone would have been ingenious enough to produce them.

Today's situation is vastly different from that of the '30s, but there are some points in common. Shelves are loaded and stores are full of goods, and at the same time there are idle workers and machines waiting for new orders to come in. The farm machinery, steel, and other industries are operating well below capacity. Why? Because there is insufficient demand for their products. The difficulty here appears to be more on the demand side than on the supply side.

The President's difficulty stems from the obvious ambivalence of his package. Despite the unbridled optimism of the early days, it is now patently clear that there is no free supply-side lunch. Unlike Maecenas' day, and unlike the situation in the early '60s when John F. Kennedy gave the U.S. economy a real shot in the arm by cutting taxes and stimulating demand, an environment of tight money and relatively high interest rates is inhospitable to rapid growth. To have achieved the administration targets would have required an unprecedented spurt in the velocity of money (the number of times the total money supply changes hands each year).

Economist Robert J. Gordon of Northwestern University calculates that for fiscal years 1980 through 1985, velocity would have to grow by an average of 6.4 percent a year under the White House scenario, compared with 3.5 percent for the past five years. That, said economist Rudolph G. Penner of the American Enterprise Institute, is "outside the spectrum of possibility."[14]

Penner's prediction was prophetic. Not only did the velocity of money not increase at the usual rate required to validate the administration's rosy forecast, it actually declined.

As the President's Council of Economic Advisers reported in February 1983: "The 1982 decline in the velocity of money—as measured by the velocity of either M1 or M2 monetary aggregates—was historically atypical. Between 1961 and 1981, M1 velocity rose at an average annual rate of 3.2 per cent, while the velocity of M2 remained essentially constant, rising at an average annual rate of 0.2 per cent. In contrast, in 1982 the velocity of M1 fell 4.9 per cent and M2 velocity fell 6.0 per cent on a fourth quarter to fourth quarter basis.

"Although some slowdown in nominal G N P growth and in inflation in 1982 was a predictable effect of tighter monetary policies, the very sharp decline actually experienced did not reflect a decrease in the growth of the monetary aggregates. Rather the exceptional severity of the slowdown in nominal G N P growth can be traced to a combination of factors that led to an unusually sharp decline in the velocity of money, that is, in the ratio of G N P to the money stock."[15]

Monetarist theory anticipates that business and labor will change their "expectations" of price rises when they are convinced that the Fed will not deviate substantially from the long-range goal of keeping increases in the money stock in line with increases in real output and that this will convince them to moderate their claims on the economy.

What monetarists did not anticipate was the "expectations" generated by a climate of fear. Faced with staggering unemployment, people with jobs decided that it was prudent to hang on to their money in case their time was next. So for a number of reasons, including fear and uncertainty of the future, the velocity of money declined and we sank into the deepest recession in fifty years.

There is no doubt that the mid-summer '82 deathbed repentance of the monetary authorities ended the decline and sparked a modest turn-around. The rate, extent, and duration of the recovery, however, will be governed by our ability to understand and compensate for the major deviations from the classical model of our economic world.

NOTES

1 MILTON and ROSE FRIEDMAN, *Free to Choose* (New York: Avon Books, 1980), p. 63.

2 *Ibid.*, p. 25.

3 *Ibid.*, p. 11.

4 SIDNEY WEINTRAUB, *Capitalism's Inflation and Unemployment Crisis*, (New York: Addison-Wesley Publishing Company, Inc., 1978), p. 104.

5 MILTON and ROSE FRIEDMAN, *op. cit.*, p. 251.

6 Annual Report of the Council of Economic Advisers, Washington, D.C., February 1982, p. 21.

7 *Ibid.*, p. 17.

8 Jerry L. Jordan is currently Dean of the Anderson School of Management at the University of New Mexico, in Albuquerque.

9 Arthur B. Laffer is an economics professor at the University of Southern California and one of President Reagan's principal advisers.

10 *Business Week*, November 3, 1980, p. 75.

11 *The Economist*, March 31, 1981, p. 55.

12 *Business Week*, January 12, 1981, p. 12.

13 *Ibid.*

14 *Business Week*, March 16, 1981, p. 27.

15 Annual Report of the Council of Economic Advisers, February 1983, p. 21.

16 *Ibid.*

6

The Bishops' Vision

If monetarism occupies the extreme right on the scale of political myopia, the vision sketched by the Catholic Bishops in their *Ethical Reflections* represents the far left. Neither extreme really qualifies as "good news to the poor."

No one should deny the Bishops their democratic right to speak out courageously on behalf of the oppressed. On the contrary, they would be unfaithful to their calling if they didn't condemn an economic crisis that affects their parishioners so deeply. The situation is indeed immoral.

The remedy set out in the Bishops' paper, however, is fuzzy, ambiguous, and contradictory. It could have been written by a theology student meeting the requirements of Political Science 101. That such early impressions can survive to adulthood in diverse men of letters is beyond comprehension.

The Bishops attribute much of the blame for the recession to structural changes due to automation and computers, the transnational nature of corporations and banks, and the increasing concentration of capital and technology in the production of military armaments. "Indeed, these structural changes largely explain the nature of the current economic recession at home and throughout the world."[1]

Anyone who believes that is in deep economic water from the outset. The buildup in armaments can be condemned as wasteful—especially when weighed against other urgent human needs. But it didn't cause the recession. Similarly, the impact of automation and computer technology and the machinations of multinational enterprises may have affected individual persons and situations, but they didn't spark the economic slowdown. The recession of 1980 – 82 was deliberately induced in a coldly calculated attempt to fight inflation by squeezing the money supply.

The Bishops appear equally unaware of the origin of the inflation that gave rise to the crisis. Their prescription for a more balanced and equitable program to stem the rate of inflation by "shifting the burden for wage controls to upper income earners and introducing controls on prices and new forms of taxes on investment income" is not arithmetically sound.[2]

When wages comprise approximately two-thirds of total costs, how can you control prices and not control wages? Especially at a time when some prices are depressed and too many companies are still losing money. Controlling the wages of executives and not the rank and file is a good political gimmick, but I would be wary of any party that made that kind of promise. Similarly, higher taxes on investment income sounds like an appealing election ploy, but the net result would be a disincentive to capital improvement and with it the extra productivity on which real wage gains for the workers are based.

The government's 6 and 5 percent wage-restraint guidelines receive negative comment. But what about the morality of demanding even 6 percent more pay for doing approximately the same amount of work as the year before? The Bishops are silent on that issue. They want to end the imposition of guidelines and call for the restoration of free collective bargaining, apparently oblivious to the possibility that abuse of that system was the single most important contributor to the inflation of the late '60s and '70s and consequently to the current malaise.

Their approach is not even-handed. They see "monopoly control of prices" as the root of inflation rather than "workers' wages, government spending and low productivity".[3] It is true that some prices are set by monopolies and oligopolies instead of market forces, but the Bishops overlook the biggest monopoly of them all—the monopoly supply of labor by big unions. It is the combined action of big labor and big business that sets the wage rates that affect the prices that determine the rate of inflation.

The Bishops display a bias in their attitude toward capital, power developments, and megaprojects. Their negativism seems out of tune with the history of the Canadian economy and the positive effects of capital and energy toward the emancipation of the working man.

During a summertime chat that I had with Gordon Henry, former mayor of Ingersol, he commented on this very point from the perspective of his own childhood. Each summer he and his brothers spent their entire "holiday" hoeing turnips. Gordon thought he would have been a super Santa Claus because he had been "hoe-hoeing" from dawn till dusk. Now most of that work is done by machines and Gord, for one, has nothing but respect and appreciation for the technological advances. The use of capital has allowed wages to rise while guaranteeing an abundance of food at prices that Gene

Whelan would say are cheap in relative terms.

Power and capital have bestowed similar benefits on the building trades. I have observed men working with both hand and power tools. The difference in output is staggering. One man with a power saw can sheet a roof in a tiny fraction of the time it would take by hand. The worker benefits from higher wages and the consumer from lower prices—thanks to capital investment and electrical energy.

Megaprojects have played a vital role in Canada's economic, social, and cultural development. The transcontinental railways pulled the country together and opened up the hinterland to immigrants looking for a fresh start; the power plant at Niagara Falls provided the energy for the carpenter's saw; the Trans Canada Pipeline brought natural gas from Western wells to heat Eastern homes and industry; and the St. Lawrence Seaway opened up our heartland to the world. These projects have contributed immeasurably to Canadian prosperity and each was capital-intensive in its time.

Today there are new megaprojects waiting for the green light. Plants to extract oil from the tar sands, pipelines to bring oil and gas from the sea, and a massive upgrading of our railroad system to speed Western products to Eastern and foreign buyers are some examples. Monumental amounts of capital are required and admittedly few direct jobs are involved once the projects are completed. But a sophisticated and complex economy can't operate without this kind of support system any more than an airplane can fly without wings.

The Bishops' appreciation of economic history and their analysis of the current crisis is disturbing enough, but I am even more skeptical of their vision of what is required to set the world of economics straight. Why would they, of all people, recommend jumping out of the frying pan into the fire?

In a Lenten address Father William R. Ryan, National Superior of English-speaking Jesuits in Canada, tagged the Bishops' analysis as implicitly neo-Keynesian.[4] But as a life-long student of political science I read it as more implicitly neo-socialist; though for the life of me I can't think of much that is new about socialism.

It is unclear whether the Bishops' penchant for labor-intensive industries and socially useful forms of production is designed to clarify or confuse. In Father Ryan's words, their paper "unnecessarily uses ideological language offensive to some and unintelligible to many."[5]

Why would an essay that starts out on a high note of concern for the poor wind up wondering aloud if we shouldn't concentrate on labor-intensive industry? Do men of the cloth think it is better or morally superior to hoe turnips by hand? It would certainly employ more people if they could find anyone desperate enough to do it. It would also guarantee that they remain poor.

The Soviet Union mops up its unemployment by such ingenious means as stationing a middle-aged lady near the elevator doors on every floor of every hotel where she hands out keys and makes mental notes of who enters which bedroom with whom. Others carry little brooms and dustpans and march down the street behind the horses just in case of accident. Employment they have and poverty they share.

We could just as easily have full employment if we really wanted to. All that is required is for everyone on unemployment insurance and welfare to report to the nearest government office for "useful" duties. They could sweep the streets by hand in summer and shovel the snow in winter. They could wash pensioners' windows, carry out parcels at super-markets, scrub public washrooms et cetera—in a Canadian-ized version of the Soviet system. But just imagine the howls from the Bishops and others if our solution was to make the unemployed undertake public tasks for the pittance that Russians get.

If the Bishops simply mean that more Canadians should be employed making textiles, shirts, shoes, and so forth, they are remarkably inconsistent. These are the products that Third World countries count on to increase their income, and as the paper correctly points out, they have three-quarters of the world's population and only one-fifth of the income. If morality and justice are to extend beyond our borders, it would seem that running up tariff barriers and banning prod-ucts from underdeveloped countries would be a giant step in the wrong direction.

The emphasis on "socially useful forms of production" is even more perplexing. Who decides what is "socially useful"? Is that a decision we make as adult individuals acting in the marketplace? Or are we children who must delegate our decision-making to a dedicated bureaucratic elite who know "what is best" for society? Past experience may provide a few clues.

A Reuter's dispatch from Moscow appeared in the August 18, 1983, edition of the *Toronto Star* under the head-ing "Fed up Soviets rap planners over plant's useless prod-ucts." "A Soviet factory complained today it had 500 workers turning out goods which nobody in the entire country wanted and said the central planning system was to blame.

"In an unusually sharp attack on the way the Soviet eco-nomic planning structure works, the factory chiefs wrote in

the Communist Party daily *Pravda* that they had been fighting for months to have their production plan altered without
success.

"The factory, in the north Caucasus, had been ordered to
turn out low-quality curtain material by central planners. But
there was no market for this any more as people now bought
only higher-grade material."[6]

The problem is as old as the history of centralized planning bureaus. In India, government officials decided they
should build a factory to make blotting paper. When production began and they realized there was no significant market,
they decreed that certain books would contain alternate
pages of print and blotting paper in order to eliminate the
surplus.

I noted a similar problem in Yugoslavia during a visit to
research a book on economics a few years ago. The increase
in output in one particular year was substantially above the
norm. When I asked the country's top economist for an
explanation, he said the answer was simple. It was the year
they produced an avalanche of produce that nobody wanted
and that was subsequently destroyed. Little wonder that the
Yugoslavs have reintroduced a significant element of private
enterprise in their socialist model.

In Canada we build executive jet airplanes. Our government and bureaucrats bet our money on Canadair and lost.
They overpaid for the plant and then borrowed heavily to
finance production. When sales lagged, they pawned two
planes off on the Armed Forces—this at a time when one
would be hard pressed to think of anything that an organization desperately short of ships, guns, and gas needed less than
two more executive jets. Still, the overriding necessity to

make the planners look better took precedence over common sense.

The difference between public and private enterprise is in the bottom line for taxpayers. If private entrepreneurs guess incorrectly about what the public will buy, they lose their money and the product is withdrawn from the market. If, on the other hand, they are right in their projections, they share the profit with the government to help finance socially useful (sometimes) expenditures in the public domain. When public planners are wrong, as in the case of the Challenger jet, taxpayers are left with the responsibility to pay interest on the money the government borrowed and lost—for generations to come.

I am not opposed to public enterprise in principle when it is required to provide a good or a service that private investors cannot or will not provide. But after the experience of having some of Canada's largest crown corporations, including Air Canada, Canadian National Railways, and Canada Housing and Mortgage Corporation, report through me to Parliament, I am convinced that the odds are 10-to-1 that public enterprise will be less efficient than private enterprise. Politicians can't resist the temptation to interfere with public companies when necessary to serve their own political ends.

Although I am addressing some of the points raised in *Ethical Reflections*, it should be clear that the eight Catholic Bishops responsible for the text are not alone in their naïveté. The Most Reverend Edward Scott, Anglican Primate of Canada, spoke in a similar vein in his welcoming address to the Vancouver assembly of the World Council of Churches. And according to the United Church *Observer* the Right Reverend Clarke MacDonald, Moderator of the United Church, "has declared his support for the strong statement of the Canadian Conference of Catholic Bishops which calls for an economic system that places people ahead of profits."[7]

The rhetoric is right out of the 1930s. It has a nice pious ring to it, but if it has any meaning in terms of economics it is "rule by a bureaucratic elite"—decision-making by the kind of people who make blotting paper, cheesecloth curtains, and executive jets. They certainly know how to eliminate profits, but it requires a lively imagination to suggest that they put people's real needs first. People who really believe in this alternative usually fall into the class of intellectuals mentioned in Chapter 1 who have observed capitalism's foibles, rejected the system on the strength of its record, but who haven't taken the trouble to analyze why the objectionable cycles have occurred.

There are churchmen who vigorously support a contrary view. In his book *The Spirit of Democratic Capitalism* U.S. theologian Michael Novak describes the shortcomings of his peers as economic-policy analysts: "They demand jobs without comprehending how jobs are created. They demand the distribution of the world's goods without insight into how the store of the world's goods may be expanded. They desire ends without critical knowledge about means. They claim to be leaders without having mastered the techniques of human progress."[8]

In Novak's view, "the invention of the market in Great Britain and the United States more profoundly revolutionized the world between 1800 and the present than any other single force."[9]

This is not the place to argue so broad a question, but there can be little doubt that any system that generates either double-digit inflation or double-digit unemployment is a system in need of repair. Like the Bishops, I cannot accept an unemployment rate of 8 or even 6 percent as either "normal" or "natural." There has to be an acceptable solution.

Emmett Cardinal Carter probably spoke for the majority of churchmen and the majority of Canadians when he applauded the committee of Bishops for their moral stand while dissociating himself from their means. That is my position exactly. Socialism has a long history of promising pie in the sky and delivering shortages. Like monetarism, it, too, is a cure worse than the disease.

Father Ryan provided a very generous interpretation of *Ethical Reflections* when he concluded that what the Bishops were really calling for was a "letting go of our 'habitual way of thinking.'" That is really my plea to them. It isn't necessary to choose between inflation and unemployment, as they suggest, and I invite them to study an analysis that leads to the conclusion that both are unnecessary—a prospect that is really good news for the poor!

NOTES

1 *Ethical Reflections on the Economic Crisis*. Episcopal Commission for Social Affairs, Canadian Conference of Catholic Bishops, Concacan Inc., 1983.
2 *Ibid*.
3 *Ibid*.
4 *Globe and Mail*, Toronto, March 10, 1983.
5 *Ibid*.
6 *Toronto Star*, August 18, 1983, p. F14.

7

The Schizo Economy

All too often people refer to Western industrialized economies, and the United States in particular, as free-enterprise economies. It is a classic misnomer and a disservice to rational argument because it conjures up the make-believe image of a pure price-competitive system. Nothing could be further from the truth.

Modern industrial economies are a mixture of small and large, public and private enterprise where some prices are determined by the law of supply and demand and others, including some of the most important ones, are not. Price-competitive enterprise operates side by side with natural monopolies, oligopolies, and trade unions where competition, to the extent that it exists, is limited and prices are inelastic. A system comprising both free and rigid sectors can be labeled a schizo economy—one where two very different kinds of enterprise must co-exist.

The President's Council of Economic Advisers points out that "a natural monopoly exists when the relevant demand for a good or service can be satisfied at the least total cost by a single firm. At the local level it is probably wasteful to have duplicate distribution systems to provide telephone, electric, gas and water services. Among industries regulated at the federal level, major gas pipelines and high-voltage electric lines are often considered natural monopolies. Long distance telephone transmission may also be a natural monopoly in areas of low density. Railroads are a potential natural monopoly only for that declining share of rail traffic for which the shipper does not have an effective choice of carrier or mode of transport."[1] The Canadian list is not too different but somewhat more extensive because of our history and low population density.

Although natural monopolies play a significant role in the economy, their power and over-all economic impact are minimal in comparison to that of the oligopolies—the inelegant name that economists have applied to situations where the market is dominated by a few sellers.

Any progressive concentration of market power is likely to end in oligopoly. The evolution of the automobile industry is a case in point. Its early history included names like Durant, Hudson, Packard, Pierce Arrow, Peerless, Thomas, and Studebaker. In the '30s the Auburn and Cord were "hot" with highway buffs. With the passing of time, however, there have been many casualties. Some companies have disappeared and others have been consolidated until today there are only four U.S. firms of significance, and the industry is dominated by three—with one of those just getting off the ropes.

Important concentrations have occurred in other industries. Markets for cereal breakfast foods, blended and prepared flour, cookies and crackers, cane and beet sugar, chocolate products, chewing gum, malt beverages, roasted coffee, cigarettes, pet food, metal cans, typewriters, greeting cards, cellulose fibers, soaps and detergents, explosives, petroleum and coal products, tires and tubes, glass, gypsum products, refrigerators and freezers, sewing machines, electric lamps, batteries, photographic equipment and supplies and myriad other products are dominated by a handful of firms. More than 50 percent of sales accrue to four or fewer companies.[2]

The fact that the concentration has not continued to the point where oligopoly is replaced by monopoly is a benefit that University of Chicago economist and Nobel laureate George Stigler attributes to antitrust laws. He argues that antitrust policies have replaced monopoly and incipient monopoly with oligopoly as the dominant industrial market structure.[3]

In *The Economics of Antitrust, Competition and Monopoly*, Richard E. Low says: "The argument can be supported by a host of historical evidence. Oil, tobacco, steel and many other leading products were produced by monopolies, or near monopolies in the early part of this century until these monopolies were dissolved by the application of antitrust suits or by the passage of time. According to Professor Stigler, and he seems to have logic on his side, time proved as effective as it did only because of the ever-present threat of antitrust. The power of monopolies and of cartels in modern economies without our antitrust policies substantiates this belief."[4]

Whether the difference between U.S. and European experience has been due to the threat of antitrust's big stick or the relative size of the markets is immaterial to most economists' belief that the oligopolies' record in pricing, output, and economic progress is far better than that of monopolies.

Even so, that is not to say that they normally engage in the kind of price competition that occurs when there are many sellers. They are far too interdependent.

Professor Richard E. Caves's description of oligopoly underscores the importance of this seller interdependence. "The essence of oligopoly is that firms are few enough to recognize the impact of their actions on their rivals and thus on the market as a whole. . . . When an industry contains one firm (monopoly) or many firms (pure competition), the individual sellers react only to impersonal market forces. In oligopoly they react to one another in a direct and personal fashion. This inevitable interaction of sellers in an oligopolistic market we call mutual interdependence. Where mutual interdependence exists, sellers do not just take into account the effects of their actions on the total markets . . . they also take into account the effects of their actions on one another. Oligopoly becomes something like a poker game."[5]

It is a game in which the stakes are too high to engage in predatory price-cutting. This rule is so entrenched that oligopolists seldom break it. When they do—as in the case of the U.S. steel industry in 1982—the self-immolation is so painful that it doesn't take long for reason to return. The suicidal discounting didn't result in either increased demand for steel or higher profit margins.

Normally, oligopolists play according to their own tacitly understood set of rules and limit competition to advertising and promotion, style changes, and product improvement. This well-understood practice was confirmed for me some years ago by a senior executive of one of the big soap companies. At a luncheon following a seminar on the subject, one of his subordinates had been dutifully denying the remotest possibility of cooperation among companies. His chief, who didn't wish to appear ridiculous in the face of a convincing case, merely said, "Let's say we have an understanding."

Of course they do. All oligopolies operate that way. Usually the understanding is implicit rather than explicit. They don't have to exchange memos to know what must be done. Their costs rise at roughly the same rate, so their prices rise to about the same level at approximately the same time. That is quite natural and oligopolies are very good at doing what comes naturally.

LABOR

If the existence of natural monopolies and oligopolies chips away at the free-market illusion, the power and the influence of the trade union movement undermine its very foundation. Combine the power of unions with that of oligopolistic and monopolistic employers and the whole concept of free-market price determination falls in ruins.

From the small, struggling craft unions the movement has grown to the point where it qualifies in its own right as big business. Not only do unions handle enormous sums of money for current operations, strike funds, and pensions, they have gained sufficient political clout to make politicians tremble. Even more important, from an economic point of view, big unions have become monopoly suppliers of labor in many of the big industries.

Admittedly, the same power does not apply in every small industry. Except in jurisdictions like Quebec, where it is now prohibited by law, it may be possible for small firms to break unions by hiring non-union workers to cross picket lines. There is no similar balance of power between big unions and big business. If the United Auto Workers decide to strike General Motors, there is no feasible way of replacing such a large and highly skilled work force from the labor market at large. A strike of that magnitude can't be broken. It will end only when one or the other side (or both) decides to cut its losses.

The consequences for the economy at large are monumental. Business is directly affected by the actions of its competitors. One generous settlement can create shock waves for the whole industry, and it matters little whether the award is related to productivity or simply the vulnerability of the target company.

Toronto's newspaper industry provides a classic example. In the fall of '81 the *Globe and Mail* opened all of its contracts and granted an extra 2 percent to all employees. The following spring it settled with its craft unions at 13 and 12 percent in a two-year contract.

The result was as predictable as summer following spring. Unions at the *Toronto Star*, Canada's largest-circulation newspaper, demanded and got a 13.4 percent increase at a time when profits were substantially below previous years, and the paper had been giving strong editorial support to the federal government's program of a voluntary 6 percent limit on settlements in the private sector.

The unions knew that the *Star* was vulnerable. Toronto is North America's most competitive newspaper market, and there is some doubt that all three dailies can survive beyond the decade. So management was faced with an impossible choice: settle for several percentage points above their best offer or face an extended strike and lose circulation that might never be recovered. In the end long-term survival dictated a strategic surrender.

The effect on the communications industry was swift. *Globe* employees whose contracts were up for renewal demanded parity. They didn't quite achieve it, but the *Star* precedent permitted them to extract several percentage points more than would have been possible otherwise. Across town, the editor of the weekly *Financial Post* immediately added about 2 percent to his budgeted labor costs for the ensuing year. Similar pressure was felt in some areas of the electronic media.

In October '83 the *Star* failed to reach an agreement with its editorial, advertising, business, delivery and circulation employees and was hit by a strike for the first time in its ninety-one-year history. The walkout ended four days later with a settlement based on 9 and 7 per cent increases over two years. Guild president John Bryant described the agreement as "a victory for both sides" and *Star* president David Jolley said he was "very happy" that the dispute had ended quickly—before there was any permanent damage to the *Star's* position in the market.

The contract must have been agreeable to both sides but it was also highly inflationary, at a time when everyone was fearful of renewed inflation, and will have far-reaching and damaging repercussions on future negotiations throughout the industry. It's a phenomenon that a number of economists, including Aubrey Jones, a former Tory cabinet minister, and later Wages and Prices Commissioner under a Labor government in the United Kingdom, have dubbed "wage leadership."[6] The most powerful union, in the most strategically advantageous position, sets the yardstick by which all subsequent negotiations are measured.

The practice is widespread in industrialized societies. *A Study of the Role of Key Wage Bargains in the Irish System of Collective Bargaining*, by W. E. J. McCarthy, J. F. O'Brien and R. G. Dowd, underlines its significance in that country. "One of the most important conclusions to emerge is that wage leadership could give rise to rapidly rising prices even if all other factors contributing to the latter process were totally neutralized. This is so because key wage claims, induced by disturbed relativities, can initiate a general upward movement in wage relativities. This vital point has never been explicitly brought out in the substantial body of statistical, economic and econometric work which has already been published concerning inflation in Ireland. The principal reason for this is that these disciplines cannot cope with the institutional dynamics which lie at the heart of the problem."[7]

That is the nut of it. The science of economics has no mathematical formula to quantify a phenomenon that is as much political and sociological as economic. A phenomenon, nevertheless, with incalculable economic consequences.

The professional economist's frustration at the intrusion of such mischievous intangibles was clear at a York University symposium in June 1982. I was making the point that Canadian Seaway workers had demanded and obtained a 30 percent increase in a two-year contract in 1965 and that the unprecedented gain was cited in subsequent negotiations all across the country.

Michael Parkin, a monetarist from the University of Western Ontario, wanted to know why the workers had asked for 30 percent rather than some greater or lesser number.[8] In this case the answer was straightforward. It wasn't internal Canadian relativities that shaped their demands but rather the comparison with U.S. Seaway workers, who were paid 30 percent more than the Canadians for performing precisely the same work. A commissioner was appointed to arbitrate and he meekly recommended that parity be granted. Then, though fully aware that acquiescence would create shock waves, a lily-livered government, of which I was a member, capitulated in order to avoid a "legislated settlement."

Although the source of the percentage increase demanded by the Seaway workers was readily apparent, this case was an exception. There is no general formula. Negotiating positions can be based on relativity with workers in the same industry, comparison with another industry, keeping up with inflation, or just what the traffic will bear.

In the United States the traditional practice in the automobile industry is a good example of how the system works. The UAW picked its "target" for negotiations, presumably the company with the most to lose from a strike; then once a settlement was agreed upon, it was used as a basis of negotiations with the other companies.

Of course, the system breaks down when an industry is in distress. Concessions granted to Chrysler Corporation were a precedent-setting departure from previous practice. Faced with the unhappy choice of either putting Chrysler into bankruptcy and losing their jobs or making pay concessions, workers gambled on keeping the company afloat. This bow in the direction of common sense should be viewed as an aberration rather than a fundamental change in approach. In an earlier draft of this chapter I suggested that, should

ɔs and company profitability increase, it
as sure as night following day that there
to re-establish parity with other auto
...en, demand and profitability have increased
...rysler workers soon made it clear that they wanted
increases to put them back in line with their brothers and sisters at G M and Ford.

The impact from the unregulated exercise of monopoly union power has not yet been incorporated into the economic equation. This results in some strange anomalies. For example, natural monopolies have their prices to consumers regulated; yet one of their principal costs is not. So wage increases, no matter how great, are just passed through to the consuming public.

I recall a former president of Bell Telephone of Canada vehemently insisting that big business was responsible enough to police its own labor settlements in a manner compatible with the public interest. Only weeks later his company signed a pace-setting agreement in order to avoid a strike. Naturally, Bell was allowed to pass the highly inflationary cost increases on to its subscribers without penalty. Not only that, the magnitude of the settlement became a benchmark for diverse service unions.

In practice, oligopolies are pretty much in the same boat. Because they have the collective market power to pass cost increases on to the consuming public, they are not responsible enough to police their own settlements. Like big labor, big business puts its own perceived short-term interests first. Consequently, many contracts are signed that appear beneficial to business or labor or both but may be detrimental to the public interest.

The 1979 agreement between General Motors and the
United Auto workers is a case in point. The contract must
have been acceptable to both parties at the time because it

Figure 4

Steel, Auto Wages Outpace the Pack

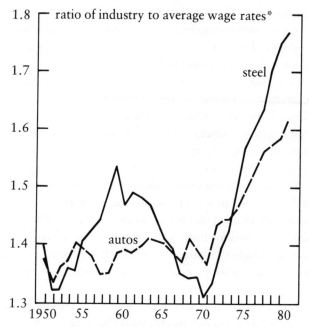

Note: Average hourly earnings of production workers in steel mills
and in motor vehicle manufacturing plants divided by
average hourly earnings of all private non-farm production
and non-supervisory workers.

Source: U.S. Bureau of Labor Statistics.

was signed without a strike. From the standpoint of the public interest, however, it was inflationary. Also, it may have been detrimental to the long-term interest of the workers themselves.

As Figure 4 illustrates, the increase in relative wages has been particularly sharp in specific cases. During the 1970s the wage rates for U.S. steel and auto workers rocketed above the pack. This startling change in relativities was out of line with underlying economic conditions and increased the vulnerability of those industries as the economy weakened and foreign competition became more intense.

Governments play a part in the uncertain wage equation too. Because they have no bottom line they have made concessions that can't be sustained in the economy at large without an increase in prices or taxes or both. Without the harness of personal financial restraint, they accede to conditions that can be met only because somebody else pays.

Whether by monopolies, oligopolies, or governments, it was the approval of wage increases well in excess of average productivity that led inexorably to an ever-higher level of underlying inflation. Each additional increase, whether in response to higher oil prices, more expensive food, or just a desire to keep up with a new record settlement, gave the spiral another twist.

It is the naïve assumption that monetary restraint will effectively and permanently eliminate the wage-leadership phenomenon that unites monetarists and classical economists. While admitting some obvious rigidities, they still insist it's just a question of time until it all comes out in the wash.

In the words of the President's Council, "If prices and

wages were perfectly flexible, reduced nominal GNP growth would translate immediately and painlessly into reduced inflation. However, not all wages and prices are flexible. When expectations of future inflation are deeply embedded, prices and wages may continue to rise for some time despite excess supplies of goods and labor. A change in inflationary expectations, together with the direct pressures exerted by excess supplies, eventually cause prices and wages to adjust to new market-clearing levels. But until that occurs a slow-down in nominal GNP growth is reflected in a slowing of real growth as well as in a slowing of inflation."[9]

THE FATAL FLAW

The assumption that all wages and prices ultimately respond to market pressure is the fatal flaw in official policy. In discussing the Fed's approach of reducing the rate of growth of the monetary aggregates, Chairman Volcker used a distinctly monetaristlike formulation. "Our policy, taken in a longer perspective, rests on a simple premise—documented by centuries of experience—that the inflationary process is ultimately related to excessive growth in money and credit."[10]

Partly true but misleading, the statement exhibits the kind of sentimental generality that leads both monetarists and non-monetarists to talk and act as if wages and prices were easily compressible like some kind of gas. Instead, these have been increasingly fossilized by various forms of monopoly power and have become more like granite.

Union strength increased through the World War II and postwar years to the point where it can shut down companies and whole industries at will, or where it often holds a company's very existence in its hands—as was dramatically demonstrated in the case of the Chrysler Corporation. The monopoly power of the unions is now virtually absolute in key sectors. They set the nominal wage level to which everyone must aspire.

Most economists are willing to admit that wages and prices are relatively insensitive to moderate slack in the economy. Governor Bouey did in his 1980 annual report, when he wrote: "It is sometimes said that the reduction of inflation in Canada through market processes is not practical in that markets are too unresponsive because of the degree to which power to control supply and prices lies in the hands of particular businesses or trade unions or marketing boards or regulatory agencies."[11]

Having admitted the obvious, Bouey blindly followed his peers in placing his reliance on the monetary tourniquet: "To the extent, however, that markets respond insensitively—to the extent that groups and markets have and use the power to continue to push up costs and prices rapidly in the face of weakening market conditions—the reduction of inflation will require a greater easing of total demand and thus a greater impact on output and employment."[12]

But at what cost? At what level of slack do they expect this magic transformation to occur? Their most recent experiment in monetary restraint, which culminated in the recession of 1981 – 83 almost wrecked the system and still prices increased. This totally unwarranted assumption that business and labor will miraculously moderate their claims to the point where costs cease to rise and full employment can be financed by simply expanding the money supply in direct proportion to the increase in physical output marks Paul Volcker, Gerald Bouey, Milton Friedman, and the tens of thousands of professors, economists, bankers, and businessmen who agree with them, as decades out of date.

To take these experts seriously, you have to believe that for all future time negotiating teams representing the most powerful trade unions will sit down at the bargaining table and say, "We'll settle for a 2 percent increase this year. We think that's about what the average increase in productivity will be." And, equally unlikely, that pacesetters like the building trades unions will say, "We're ready to sign a two-year contract with a 1 percent increase each year. We've moved a bit ahead of the pack and we would like to see the poor given a little break, so we'll share our increase in productivity with them for a couple of years, to help them get their heads above water."

If, deep down, you honestly believe that is likely to happen, then monetarism is your game. Stop here. If, on the other hand, you are skeptical and harbor real doubts, read on.

NOTES

1 Annual Report of the Council of Economic Advisers, Washington, D.C., February 1983, p. 98.
2 1972 Census of Manufacturers, *Concentration Ratios in Manufacturing* (Washington D.C.: U.S. Department of Commerce, 1975), pp. 6 – 46.
3 GEORGE J. STIGLER, "Monopoly & Oligopoly by Merger," *American Economic Review Supplement*, XL (1950), pp. 23 ff.

4 RICHARD E. LOW, ed., *The Economics of Antitrust, Competition and Monopoly* (Englewood Cliffs, N.J.: Prentice-Hall Inc., 1968), p. 6.

5 RICHARD E. CAVES, *American Industry: Structure, Conduct, Performance*, 2nd ed. (Englewood Cliffs, N.J.: Prentice-Hall Inc., 1968), p. 6.

6 AUBREY JONES, *The New Inflation* (London: Andre Deutsch and Penguin Books, 1973).

7 W.E.J. MCCARTHY, J.F. O'BRIEN, V.G. DOWD, *Wage Inflation and Wage Leadership: A Study of the Role of Key Wage Bargains in the Irish System of Collective Bargaining* (Dublin: Cahill & Co. Ltd., 1975).

8 See *Prospects for Man: Economics, Inflation and Unemployment*, W.J. Megaw, ed. (a symposium presented by the Faculty of Science, York University).

9 Annual Report of the Council of Economic Advisers, February 1983, pp. 20 – 21.

10 *Business Week*, March 31, 1980, p. 80.

11 Bank of Canada 1980 Annual Report, Ottawa, March 1982, p. 7.

12 *Ibid.*

8

Wages Out of Joint with Productivity

It is a central thesis of this book that the widening gap between wage increases and productivity was the predominant source of the inflation of the '70s and early '80s. Higher labor unit costs pushed prices up. Then the attempt to stop the cycle by means of monetary strangulation produced stagflation and indecent levels of unemployment.

Most economists recognize that there is a relationship between wages and prices. The President's Council of Economic Advisers was right on target in its January 1981 report in saying: ". . . since payments to labor are estimated to account for almost two-thirds of total production costs, prices over the long term tend to move in conjunction with changes in labor unit costs."[1]

Precisely! In the longer term, prices move up at a rate that approximates the increase in wages and fringe benefits minus the increase in output per person. Simply stated, inflation will be approximately equal to wage increase minus productivity.

While economists admit the connection between wages and prices, when it comes to giving reasons for the wage-price spiral they are like politicians—each has his own opinion. As stated earlier, many believe that it began with the Vietnam war and gained impetus from food shortages and the big oil price increases. But this widely held view doesn't hold water when examined from the wider perspective of experience in other countries. Wage escalation occurred long before the effects of the Vietnam war could be felt. As early as 1961, wages shot upward in Austria, Denmark, Italy, Japan, and Sweden. A year later it was Ireland's turn, followed by Canada and the United Kingdom in 1964. It was 1965 before the United States joined the parade. So it is slightly absurd to attribute an established international phenomenon to the Vietnam conflict.

Disagreement concerning the origin of the wage-price spiral is exceeded only by apparent uncertainty as to which came first, the chicken or the egg. Businessmen know which comes first. Anyone who has made and sold a product or marketed a service knows that pricing begins by adding up the costs, including labor, and then adding a margin of profit. When the cost of labor rises faster than productivity, prices must rise. There are cases where a brisk demand may permit a higher markup or a slack demand may dictate a lower one; but inevitably the pricing mechanism begins by covering costs. Published data show that this is the sequence. Figure 5 illustrates the ups and downs of wage increases in Italy over a twenty-year period, including the steep rise in 1961, and shows how prices tend to tag along behind.

The reason that wages have been able to outpace productivity is "power." Trade unions have the power to extract increases in excess of productivity, and big business and big government have the ability to pass the increased costs along to consumers and taxpayers by means of higher prices and

Figure 5
Average Annual Increase in Wages and Prices, Italy, 1959 – 1981

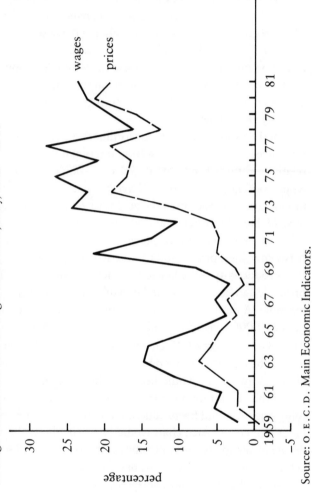

Source: O. E. C. D. Main Economic Indicators.

higher taxes. The restraint of Adam Smith's "invisible hand" doesn't apply in many key sectors of the economy.

Milton Friedman acknowledged that fact when he discussed the danger implicit in unions' demand for a say in the editorial content of newspapers. Relating the case of *The London Times*, and the union's success in shutting it down, Friedman put his finger on the most profound development in modern economics: "The unions in question are able to exercise this power because they have been granted special immunities by government."[2]

In the exercise of their extraordinary power unions are influenced by factors ranging from internal politics to wage relativities. Little heed is paid to the question of productivity, while nominal wage increases have become a matter of paramount concern. Too often the goal is to get more and give less. We have forgotten that the only way we can all get more is to give more. The public perception of the connection between wages, prices, and productivity is very fuzzy.

Productivity is the key to real increases in income. The principle can be expressed in layman's terms in this simple example. A master craftsman employed in a speciality shop is paid $10,000 a year for producing 100 hand-carved chairs. The labor unit cost of the chairs is $100 each. If, for some reason, he decided to spend his entire income to purchase his own handiwork, he would be able to buy 100 chairs.

If the same tradesman insisted on a 10 percent raise the following year, and his production remained constant, the labor unit cost of each chair would be $110. Should he again decide to spend his entire income on chairs, he would only get the same 100 chairs for his new salary of $11,000.

If, on the other hand, he agreed to a 3 percent wage hike

Figure 6
Indexes of Productivity: Real and Nominal Weekly Wages, Commercial Non-agricultural Industries, Canada, 1966 – 1980

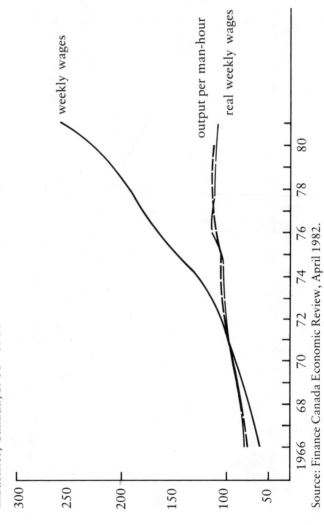

Source: Finance Canada Economic Review, April 1982.

Figure 7
Indexes of Productivity: Real and Nominal Compensation, Private Non-farm Industries,
United States, 1966–1981

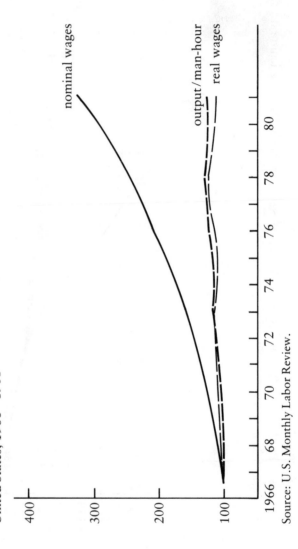

nominal wages

output/man-hour

real wages

400

300

200

100

1966   68   70   72   74   76   78   80

Source: U.S. Monthly Labor Review.

and at the same time increased his output to 103 chairs a year, the labor unit cost would remain constant at $100. In that case, should he decide to spend his total income on his own product, he would be able to buy 103 with his salary of $10,300.

Needless to say, I have omitted all other costs—including materials, energy, and overhead—in order to avoid complications that are less important than the main point. The principal message, which is loud and clear, is that there is no connection whatsoever between nominal wages—the amount of money in your pay envelope—and what they will buy.

The graphs in Figures 6 and 7 show that there is no correlation between nominal and real compensation. On the other hand, there is a very direct and close relationship between real output and real wages. The two follow each other closely. The slight decline in real wages beginning about 1974 would appear to reflect a change in income shares because of the dramatic increase in oil prices. The great recession also played havoc with real wages.

What is true for hourly or weekly wages and output is equally true for annual wages and output. The reason Japanese workers have enjoyed such a large increase in real wages is simply that their productivity has been so far above average. The annual growth in Gross National Product per employed worker for the decade 1963 – 73 was 8.4 percent for Japan, compared with 2.0 percent for the United States and 2.5 percent for Canada. Comparable figures for the 1973 – 79 period were Japan 2.9, the United States 0.1, and Canada 0.2 percent.

The statistics for average increases in productivity camouflage the remarkable ranges between one industry and another. In the decade ending in 1977 the index of productivity for synthetic fibers more than doubled in the United States, and substantial gains were registered in many other industries, such as air transport and pharmaceutical preparations. The index for retail food stores, on the other hand, increased just marginally, while productivity in coal mining had actually fallen.

Productivity rates in many of the service industries are relatively static. It's not easy for a policeman to cover a wider beat, for preachers to increase their visitations, or even for columnists to produce more words without diminishing the quality. In some cases, efforts to increase productivity are actually negative. When the number of pupils per class is reduced to permit more individual attention, productivity, as it is measured in economics, declines. The medical profession is a classic example. If, through the use of increasingly advanced techniques, the number of doctors and nurses required for an operation is greater, productivity, as we measure it, is less. This is not a measure of quality. The social benefits from higher standards are real, but they are difficult to measure and cannot be translated into disposable income. Therefore they are excluded from this analysis, where the important point is that productivity rates, as we measure them, vary enormously.

The consequences of lower-than-average productivity rates were recognized by the President's Council of Economic Advisers: "Medical care costs have added significantly to inflation for most of the past decade. Except for the period of mandatory wage-price controls from 1971 through early 1974, medical care costs have risen much more rapidly than other prices. From 1973 through 1977 the cost of medical care rose at an average annual rate of 10.2 per cent, compared to 7.7 per cent for the total Consumer Price Index."[3]

Inflation gets a boost when a group of workers in an industry with a relatively high productivity rate bargain for a proportionate increase in wages. In some industries, such as synthetic fibers, an 8 percent increase might be justified on the basis of increased productivity, and granted without the necessity of either a higher price for the product or lower profits. But what about the people employed in the service industries? Are their wages to remain forever frozen because their output is either constant or declining from one year to the next? Or should they be entitled to some share of the benefits from the use of additional capital and improved technology?

Human nature being what it is, a demand for big wage increases, like the common cold, is catching. One group of workers is influenced by another. As Aubrey Jones explained in *The New Inflation*, each will covet the highest gain that can be justified by historical relationships or other yardsticks. Wages, like water, seek their own level—the level set by the highest relevant settlement. If the general level of wage settlements flows from the leadership of either the most productive or the most powerful, then obviously the attempts of other groups in society to keep up or catch up will be highly inflationary. Experience has shown that teachers, public servants, doctors, nurses, inspectors, and others will not accept settlements that seriously alter the pecking order between their wages and those of industrial workers. Yet to the extent that their increases are not offset by increases in productivity, they can only be paid by printing more money.

CONTEMPORARY INFLATION: P = W – Q

It appears clear from the foregoing that, other things being equal, the rate of change in the price level will approximate the difference between the average rate of change in money wages, including fringe benefits, and the average rate of change in the production of goods and services. Stating this symbolically, we have $P = W - Q$ where P is the rate of change in the price level, W is the average rate of change in money wages, and Q is the average rate of change in real output of goods and services per worker in the labor force.

The assumptions include reasonable levels of employment. The definition varies from country to country, but for my purposes it is the condition that would be considered "normal" at the time. Another condition is a neutral monetary policy. This assumes that the money stock will be changed at a rate that will neither "overheat" nor "cool" the economy. The third assumption is that domestic prices are not unduly influenced by imports—that in fact import prices are rising at a rate more or less comparable to domestic prices.

Of course $P = W - Q$ is an imprecise formula—especially in the short run—because its accuracy depends on assumptions that seldom apply for extended periods. But if one looks at the data for a group of fourteen O.E.C.D. (Organization for Economic Co-operation and Development) countries shown in Table 1 the long-term result for most countries is close. The over-all average of averages is amazingly accurate—within one-quarter of 1 percent over a twenty-two year period.[4] A correlation that close is very convincing!

TABLE 1

Prices, Wages, and Productivity for 14 O.E.C.D. Countries

	(1)	(2)	(3)	(4)	(5)
	P	W	Q	W–Q	Difference Between 1 & 4
Austria	4.6	9.2	4.7	4.5	0.1
Belgium	4.8	9.7	3.5	6.2	–1.4
Canada	5.0	7.6	1.6	6.0	–1.0
Denmark	6.9	12.0	2.6	9.4	–2.5
France	6.7	10.8	3.8	7.0	–0.3
Germany	3.7	8.1	4.5	3.6	0.1
Ireland	8.4	12.9	3.9	9.0	–0.6
Japan	7.0	12.4	7.0	5.4	1.6
Netherlands	5.3	8.8	3.4	5.4	–0.1
Norway	6.0	9.6	3.1	6.5	–0.5
Sweden	6.2	8.8	2.4	6.4	–0.2
Switzerland	3.8	5.5	2.6	2.9	0.9
U.K.	8.2	10.7	2.3	8.4	–0.2
U.S.A.	4.8	5.8	1.7	4.1	0.7
Aggregate Average	5.81	9.42	3.36	6.06	0.25

Source: O.E.C.D. Main Economic Indicators, 1960–80.

      O.E.C.D. National Accounts—Labor Force Statistics.

It is a travesty to believe that the real cost of labor gains comes from the employer's pocket. It might, in the short run. But in the long run, because the division of the economic pie between capital and labor changes so gradually, the full cost of all wasteful practices, and of increased benefits such as shorter working hours, is borne by all of us, collectively, as consumers and as workers.

Consequently, intelligent trade unionism should be largely unconcerned with nominal wages. It should be very much concerned with productivity and should turn its full attention to the source of real wage gains. That means that it should fight to eliminate featherbedding wherever it occurs because every time a union resists automation in producing a newspaper, sorting mail, or in any one of a thousand other ways, the real purchasing power of all wages is held down a little bit. Every time hours of work are shortened (without a compensating increase in productivity), every time coffee breaks are lengthened or male maternity leave is granted, the cost of doing business rises and the value of real wages declines. Every strike, lockout, or work-to-rule campaign plays havoc with productivity and consequently with the real value of pay.

It should be clear from the evidence that the dramatic break in the link between productivity and incomes which accelerated in the '60s and on through the '70s was the principal cause of the inflation of this period—and indirectly, through the application of misguided cures, the origin of stagflation and economic chaos. Unions with a monopoly supply of labor in key industries were the pace-setters. Others joined the race in an attempt to keep up.

Of course, unions couldn't have done what they have without the special immunities of which Friedman spoke. Nor could they have done it without the acquiescence of their equally influential employers. Together, their power and influence in the economic world are enormous. They are like giant whales thrashing around in a pool with smaller species ranging in size from barracudas to minnows. Every twist, turn, or flip of the tail sends shock waves hurtling through the water.

NOTES

1 Annual Report of the Council of Economic Advisers, Washington, D.C., January 1981, p. 34.

2 MILTON and ROSE FRIEDMAN, *Free to Choose* (New York: Avon Books, 1980), p. 60.

3 Annual Report of the Council of Economic Advisers, January 1979, p. 45.

4 Organization for Economic Co-operation and Development, Main Economic Indicators, 1960 – 1980. *Note*: Wages 1959 – 80 except for Sweden (1960 – 80), Switzerland (1958 – 67, 1970 – 80); Prices 1959 – 80 except for Sweden (1961 – 80).

9

The Economist's Dilemma

When the imperfections in the so-called "free market" are so obvious, it is a wonder that they weren't fully taken into account long ago. We must prefer the comfortable clichés of our youth to the series of intellectual shocks implicit in embracing the shape of the real world around us. Like the Bishops of Rome when faced with Galileo's preposterous notion that the earth revolves about the sun, we feel safer clinging to the "universe" we know.

The conflict between faith and facts is a problem that economics and religion have in common. Anyone who believes that the world was made in six days is likely to be impervious to the implications of different ages of rocks. Similarly, adherence to the concept of pure market economics is an article of faith. To question it is heresy, even in the face of evidence to the contrary.

Most economists of the classical theology do recognize the existence of imperfections in the marketplace, but their response is archaic and grossly inadequate. It ranges from the largely ineffective antitrust to the equally uncertain deregulation approach to the market power exercised by big business. And on the even more important question of labor monopolies, they just hide their heads in the sand.

The antitrust approach dates from the second half of the nineteenth century and the rise of industrial combinations associated with names such as Rockefeller, Mellon, and Carnegie. Introduction of the Sherman Antitrust Act in 1890 was an attempt to cope with the "new beast strangling the country." The language of the new law was very broad—so broad, in fact, that high-priced lawyers found cracks a mile wide. To close the gaps the Clayton and Federal Trade Commission Acts extended the prohibition of monopolies and attempts to monopolize to include specific steps such as price discrimination, exclusive contracts, acquisition of stock in a competing corporation, and any undefined "unfairness" that might lessen competition. More recently, the Celler-Kefauver Anti-Merger Act proscribed mergers that might promote monopoly. This plugged a loophole that allowed a firm to buy a competitor's assets even though acquisition of its stock was forbidden.

In 1968 Columbia University economics professor Donald Dewey concluded that the original law had been passed in haste and received with some suspicion and much indifference by lawyers and economists, but he noted that "seventy-four years later the Sherman Act and its leading amendments command the support of all save a few of the surviving domestic Marxists. Antitrust litigation has created its own vested interest in the form of an industry which now provided a livelihood for hundreds of lawyers, economists, civil servants, and private detectives."[1]

Antitrust may have spawned one of America's more interesting growth industries, but more pertinent is whether it does the job intended. As I mentioned earlier, economist George Stigler argues that U.S. antitrust policies have been successful in replacing monopoly and incipient monopoly with oligopoly as the dominant force in market structure. Economists who "believe oligopoly to be economically progressive and to approach purely competitive pricing and output,"[2] as Professor Richard E. Low describes them, consider this to be a revolutionary development and one of great political significance.

I am extremely doubtful of claims that oligopolies "approach purely competitive pricing and output." In my experience, price competition has been the exception rather than the rule. This was predicted by the great "trust buster" Theodore Roosevelt, who ridiculed the impossible task of restoring flintlock conditions of competition by trusting only to a succession of lawsuits. Adam Smith was equally prescient when he said: "People of the same trade seldom meet together, even for merriment and diversion, but the conversation ends in a conspiracy against the public, or in some contrivance to raise prices. It is impossible to prevent such meetings, by any law which either could be executed, or would be consistent with liberty and justice."[3]

This is the point I have been arguing. Oligopolists don't sign agreements to set prices; they do it over tea. Frederick T. Knickerbocker describes how the game of oligopolistic chess is played: "So long as aggressive moves provoke defensive moves, rivalry among oligopolists can potentially deteriorate into mutually destructive competition. The classic example of this is price warfare. Each firm underprices its rivals to the point where no firm in the industry can earn a profit. Oligopolists are well aware that such rivalry is a game where nobody wins."[4]

Consequently, they reach an understanding, either explicit or implicit, to avoid cutthroat competition. They maintain order in the market. Each firm restrains its aggressive behavior in the expectation that rivals will do likewise. That means shying away from price competition and concentration on advertising and product development that helps to maintain or increase its market share while simultaneously promoting demand for the benefit of the industry as a whole.

The difficulty with this interpretation, which is one I believe to be substantially correct, is the conflict between principle and practice—the gulf between the way things should be and the way they are. This intellectual conflict led historian Richard Hofstadter to observe: "The Progressive discussion of the so-called Trust or Monopoly is . . . filled with all that uneasiness and inconsistency which we may expect to see when men find themselves enmeshed in institutions and practices that seem to be working to considerable effect, but that violate their inherited precepts and their moral preferences."[5]

Canadian anti-combines law is a farce. It is embedded in the criminal law so there can be no doubt about Ottawa's jurisdiction; thus prosecutors must prove to the toughest legal standards that company executives have conspired to set prices or carve up markets. Not only that; the government has to prove that competition was "lessened unduly" as a result—a concept that is not defined in law but which has been rigidly interpreted by the courts.

Consequently, Ottawa was unable to get a conviction against three big sugar companies charged with restricting competition.[6] And, more recently, it declined to prosecute the big multinational oil companies even though an eight-year investigation alleged massive overcharging by the industry. The law simply doesn't have the teeth required to cope with industrial practices.

Faced with substantial evidence that antitrust and anticombines laws haven't accomplished their intended purpose, orthodox economists are urging that the clock be turned back so that competition is restored by means of even tougher laws and other "structural" changes. American experiments in deregulation are cited as bold examples of what can be done.

"In several industries—railroads, trucking, airlines, energy, telecommunications, banking—where the existing regulatory structures have largely outlived their usefulness, this Administration has achieved significant reform," claimed President Carter's Council of Economic Advisers.[7] President Reagan has pursued the deregulation approach with even greater ardor. His Council devoted a whole chapter to the subject in their 1983 report.[8] Still, the examples of positive long-term benefits from deregulation are limited and already some doubts have been raised by the experience of the airline industry. Deregulation brought stiffer competition and lower fares, but it also brought bankruptcies and proved once again that businesses cannot operate indefinitely without profits.

The survivors, fewer in number, must have wondered who would be next if the dog-eat-dog competition continued. They decided that enough is enough. "At least that's what American Airlines—and the rest of the industry—is saying about the thousands of post-deregulation discount fares that have left the airlines hungry for profits. American, trying to take advantage of increased traffic, introduced new fares that tie ticket prices to the distance travelled, a system that will double the fares on many routes. United Airlines was quick to follow, as were T W A and Continental. The new fare structure is nearly identical—not to mention higher—than the one in effect before deregulation."[9] The truce was fragile, however, and by the fall of 1983, discounting was back in vogue.

The future of the industry appeared bleak and Continental was in serious financial difficulty.

Canada has adopted a much more cautious attitude toward deregulation. Our government has consistently refused to open up the border to the kind of competitive free-for-all that the Americans have been demanding. The Canadian Transport Commission has also been sticky about approving discount fares advertised by Air Canada, CP Air, and other airlines for travel between points within Canada. This reluctance has caused so much confusion and inconvenience that on September 27, 1983, Transport Minister Lloyd Axworthy ordered a public inquiry into domestic air fare policy.

Milton Friedman offers another alternative to the danger of monopoly power: "The most effective way to counter it is not through a bigger antitrust division at the Department of Justice or a larger budget for the Federal Trade Commission, but through removing existing barriers to international trade. That would permit competition from all over the world to be even more effective than it is now in undermining monopoly at home. Freddie Laker of Britain needed no help from the Department of Justice to crack the airline cartel. Japanese and German automobile manufacturers forced American manufacturers to introduce smaller cars."[10]

Alas, the theory is fine but the practice is unreliable. The big boys finally caught up with Freddie Laker, and his current occupation of making television commercials is a sobering footnote to Friedman's panacea. People Express is attempting to carry on where Laker left off but is running into opposition from such a stout defender of private enterprise as Britain's Margaret Thatcher. One wishes the little company well while not banking too heavily on its success, should it become too great a threat to the established airlines.

No democratically elected government is going to allow untrammeled foreign competition if the cost in domestic jobs and votes is too high. Even the foreign car manufacturers that Friedman applauded for putting American industry on its mettle have been jaw-boned into establishing higher cost assembly plants in the United States.

In 1982 General Motors opened up competitive bidding for steel products, but when efficient Canadian producers undercut U.S. prices someone persuaded GM to backtrack and pay a premium for domestic steel. The "Buy America" provision has effectively blocked the use of Canadian cement in the giant U.S. road-improvement program. And quotas have been set on the import of Canadian beef, to the discomfort of producers and the potential benefit of Canadian consumers.

Canada plays the same game. We ask the Japanese to limit the flow of cars and use highly questionable customs procedures to restrict entry if they refuse to comply. We establish a commission to recommend that much of the content of all foreign cars be made in Canada. We establish quotas on the import of shirts and shoes in order to keep low-cost produce out and protect jobs that would otherwise be lost—for purely political reasons.

These examples are merely illustrative, the list could go on and on. Free trade is a beautiful ideal, and a long-term goal that is worth pursuing. But it is sheer folly to pretend that the pace can be one that will provide the kind of price competition that prevents big business and big labor from pushing up costs and prices. The minute the "invisible hand" of foreign competition gets too heavy to be politically bearable, someone is going to rap it over the knuckles.

Experiments designed to both increase competition and reduce trade barriers are welcome and worthwhile, but it is pure fantasy to envisage a society where unlimited price competition becomes the rule with big business. Political reality suggests that it isn't going to happen.

It must have been an earlier quest for votes that persuaded politicians not to let economic principles interfere with expediency when it came to the question of including unions in anticombines legislation. At one time, of course, they were included because they were considered to be associations in restraint of trade. But in both Canada and the United States they were subsequently excluded from the legislation.

I have no quarrel with that decision in the time frame in which it was made—not that unions weren't associations in restraint of trade, but because workers were still the underdogs and needed additional freedom and clout in their uphill battle with business. Workers suffered mightily from the recurrence of business cycles and the freedom from legal harassment provided them greater scope in redressing the historic imbalance of power. Over time, however, the net result has been the enshrinement of one of the most revered of our sacred cows: free collective bargaining. It too, has become an article of faith, a fundamental right. To suggest that there is nothing free in the way bargaining is conducted between big business and big labor is not just heresy; it is monumental heresy. Yet "free collective bargaining" is a funny way to describe "going to the mat" with an opponent.

What does the word "free" have in common with the

exercise of brute force? Not much, if one examines how the adversarial system has been working. Isn't it incongruous that, in a society where disputes of every other kind are settled in accordance with the rule of law, with a right of appeal to the courts, there should be one anachronism, one kind of dispute settled by the law of the jungle?

The whole idea is anathema to liberalism in its broadest and best sense. John Stuart Mill said that the rights of any one individual or group end at the point where they begin to trespass on the rights of another individual or group. Consequently, strikes that affect third-party interests, as most do, are a denial of freedom to those people. Citizens at large have just as much right to enjoy uninterrupted police and fire protection and power, sanitary, postal, and other services as any other group has to deny them.

The right to strike, then, is less fundamental than its advocates claim. It has become a right only because proponents have said it is, and no one has said them nay. Indeed, the "right" to strike is, in fact, a privilege granted by legislation. Its purpose was to offset employers' self-given right to lock out, and to give workers some muscle at a time when the barons of industry often treated employees like so much dirt.

Over the decades the pendulum has swung some distance in the other direction, and much of the original justification for this particular check and balance is no longer valid. Try to alter that privilege on the basis of changed circumstances, however, and you run headlong into the bishops of labor. They need to be convinced that the economic world is no longer flat, as it appeared in the 1930s. One can readily understand why labor leaders will be slow to capitulate. After all, any restriction on collective bargaining will reduce their leverage and with it the scope for internal politics in the trade union movement.

Economists have no equally acceptable alibi. They should be shouting from the rooftops that collective bargaining, as we have known it, is outmoded—that it will retard economic recovery and perpetuate the traditional tradeoff between inflation and unemployment. Instead, they have been silent on the issue while their credibility eroded.

Dian Cohen, one of Canada's more lucid economists, pinpoints the beginning of the decline in her June 13, 1983, column in *Maclean's*: "Suddenly, in 1974, we had what Western economists had previously said could never happen—the coexistence of rising inflation, shrinking economic output and growing unemployment." Since then "economists have yet to explain why theories that made so much sense 15 years ago make such little sense today".[11]

In his recent book *Dangerous Currents: The State of Economics*, Lester C. Thurow rakes his colleagues over the coals for adhering to the traditional price-auction model of the economy and then exonerates them from responsibility for the poor performance of recent years by shifting the blame to politicians. His argument is less than convincing. He attributed much of the 2.4 percent rise in the 1978 inflation rate to government action in reintroducing a system of agricultural support prices, increasing Social Security benefits, adopting trigger pricing to protect the American steel industry, and raising the minimum wage to help low-wage workers. "Other exogenous 'bad luck' factors were also at work—a rise in meat prices, a falling dollar—but government caused more than half of the 'increase' in the inflation rate that occurred from 1977 to 1978." Thurow added that "this did not happen because the Carter economists were stupid or because they did not know the effect of their policies. The government was simply trying to raise the incomes of particular groups in our society."[12]

If Thurow is correct, the government contributed 1.2 of the 7.7 percent total increase in consumer prices. At the same time he totally ignored the 5.3 percent underlying inflation rate caused by wages rising faster than productivity. How serious is an analysis that blazes all guns on the rabbit while the moose grazes on, undisturbed?

Fifty years ago John Maynard Keynes wrote that he hoped economists would someday be as competent and useful as dentists. The evidence suggests that day has yet to come. In *Dangerous Currents* Thurow demonstrates his skill as an economic surgeon. He dissects the conventional wisdom of his peers and their affection for the price-auction model of economics with a very sharp knife. But when the operation is over, sundry parts of *Homo economicus* are left lying at random on the table. Thurow neither sews the pieces back together nor provides instructions for reassembling the corpse and breathing new life into it.

This professional trait of "butcher" over "builder" was dramatically illustrated at the Conference Board of Canada's "Business Outlook for 1984" assembly at the Toronto Hilton Harbour Castle Hotel on September 28 – 29, 1983. Billed as "Fighting for a Strong Recovery," it might more appropriately have been titled "A Wake for Hope in Conventional Economics."

The Board's chief economist, Tom Maxwell, set the tone with his medium-term 1983 – 88 forecast. In his opinion the economic recovery probably reached its peak in '83; the rate of growth will be off sharply in '85 and '86 and then rebound slowly; inflation will remain in the 4 – 6 percent range; double-digit unemployment will persist at the 10 – 12 percent level; and there will be no measurable growth in real wages until 1987, when the magnificent sum of 0.7 percent should be realized. It was enough to make one weep!

Maxwell was followed by J. Richard Zecher, Senior Vice-President and Chief Economist of Chase Manhattan Bank, who reported that the U.S. outlook was not significantly better. He considered the 1983 performance about normal for a first-year recovery in the United States. But he predicted that 1984 will be less than normal for a second post-recession year. Worse, he feared that inflation, which he expected to be about 4.1 percent in '83, could rise to 6.5 percent in 1984.

John Grant, Director and Chief Economist for Wood Gundy, was less pessimistic but just enough to dissuade his clients from selling their common shares and booking a slow boat to China. A fourth panelist, M.I.T. economics professor Morris Adelman, speaking directly on the impact of falling oil prices, merely confirmed that both price and the supply of oil should be included in the long list of future uncertainties.

I was struck by the clinical nature of the discussion. There was no moral outrage at the prospect of unemployment remaining outrageously high as far ahead as one can see. There was no remorse about the role that economists had played in leading the Western world down the garden path to recession. Above all, there was no blueprint for getting us out of the mess.

Other economists may quibble about the details of Maxwell's forecast and many have. Finance Minister Marc Lalonde contradicted the Conference Board's gloomy view. But no one has been bold enough to say that inflation is cured and that employment will rise to acceptable levels. Most economists are hedging their bets and masking their confusion by talking about new and higher levels of "natural" unemployment. A few, including several top Washington economists I have talked to, sing an optimistic tune for public consumption but privately admit that they don't know what they are doing.

If there is a consensus it is that high interest rates are the biggest fly in the ointment of recovery. They have to come down by several additional percentage points for sustained growth. This isn't happening because of huge government deficits and the fear of renewed inflation. So despite the hope for some modest decline in late '83 and early '84, economists predict that interest rates could rise again in late '84 as inflation picks up steam and the Fed is obliged to clamp down on monetary expansion.

As Tom Maxwell explained, this leads us into a trap. Apart from higher taxes, which would slow the recovery, the deficit can't be reduced without growth in the private sector. Meanwhile robust growth in the private sector is unlikely until interest rates come down substantially—interest rates that won't come down due to the size of the deficits. It's a real catch-22 situation!

If you take the economists at their word, there are only two possible courses of action: either slash the deficits or eliminate the fear of renewed inflation. Of the two it is difficult to decide which is the more dubious.

Higher taxes, as Maxwell pointed out, would retard the

recovery temporarily by reducing aggregate demand. It's another case of short-term pain to achieve long-term gain. But it's largely an academic proposition because realistically neither the U.S. nor Canadian governments are likely to raise taxes substantially in an election year.

Cuts in expenditure are equally unlikely. In Canada, government outlays are actually being increased in several areas ranging from a reorganization of the Atlantic fishery through to job creation schemes of diverse sorts. South of the border, the President refuses to cut back military expenditures because he is committed to them and his right-wing constituency would be alarmed by any sudden change of direction. At the same time the Democrats, who control the Congress, won't cut social programs further for fear of alienating their traditional left-wing support. So hope of substantially lower deficits has pretty well evaporated, at least for now.

That leaves the inflation front as the only economic war game in town. Here, too, the prospects are bleak in terms of the conventional wisdom. I was disappointed but not surprised that after writing off the possibility of an early reduction in deficits, the Conference Board panelists just ignored the inflation factor in interest rates. It was just assumed that inflation will rebound with the recovery and that nothing much can be done about it.

This is the point at which most economists are lost in the wilderness. All of their main-line theories rely on monetary means to curb wage settlements. Consequently, any attempt to wrestle inflation to the ground by keeping the lid on wages would only lead to yet another recession widely predicted for 1985 and 1986.

The blind spot was illustrated by Chase Manhattan's Zecher. When he predicted that U.S. inflation will rise again in late '84, he said the reason is that "negotiating labor contracts in a period of growth is different than in a period of recession."

Truer words were never spoken! Zecher implicitly recognized union power as the engine of the wage-price spiral. But having correctly diagnosed the problem, he failed to provide any remedy. He didn't even include the item on his list of "real problems," about which there is no dialogue. These were limited to the "incomprehensible" U.S. tax system, which discriminates against investment and savings and the percentage of G N P that governments take from the taxpayers—both important questions but not comparable to the one he omitted.

Lester Thurow drives in the same lane. In *Dangerous Currents* he devotes all of two paragraphs to the role of unions in the economy. He admits that they "must be taken into account by economic theory that seeks to model reality,"[13] but then conveniently skips on to the next subject without confronting that reality. It's almost as if the subject were too big or too difficult to confront.

Yet if lower interest rates are the key to recovery, there is no alternative but to face the issue head on. Economists are obsessed with the dilemma of real interest rates at historic highs. Yet incredible as it may seem, there is virtually no discussion of the combined effect of inflation and taxation. Real rates are high by historical standards. But net rates to investors, after deducting both inflation and taxes, are less attractive. Consequently, long-term interest rates are likely to remain high until fear of renewed inflation is curbed.

With inflation forecast in the 6 percent range, a 12 percent interest coupon may appear superficially very attractive. It is for someone who pays no taxes. But for someone in the 33 percent tax bracket the net yield is only 2 percent, while for anyone in the 50 percent tax bracket the net yield is 0 percent—hardly high by any standard, historical or otherwise. And certainly not high enough to encourage investment. Sustained inflation is new to economists who haven't yet learned that mention of "real rates" while ignoring taxes is a nonsense.

Although it is theoretically possible to eliminate the tax on inflationary increments, it is an extremely complicated proposition. It is just as easy and in the long run much more desirable to eliminate inflation, in which case the problem solves itself.

Inflation can quickly be brought under control and fear of renewed inflation eliminated by tying union wages to average productivity. Then, as inflation subsides, interest rates can be safely reduced to levels that will stimulate growth in interest-sensitive industries such as housing, automobiles, farm machinery, and durable goods of all kinds. It would also encourage capital investment which is marginal or uneconomic at current interest rates. Increased economic growth and higher employment would generate the revenues to reduce government deficits, which in turn would provide further relief from the pressure on interest rates. This is not only the fairest way; it is the only way I know of to escape from stagflation's trap.

Despite this truism, too many economists remain less than realistic. They refuse to accept the implications of recognizing oligopolies and monopoly labor as permanent features of a sophisticated, technologically advanced economy either because they don't want to face the legal and economic adjustments that flow from the admission or because their sensibilities are offended by the thought.

The free-market approach implies that all giant corporations would be broken up so that the component parts would compete fully with one another. Also that trade unions would be disbanded, with labor content to accept whatever wages were offered in the marketplace. Apart from the debatable advantages of such a policy, the odds of this happening in any democratic society where men have to get elected is about the same as picking up thirteen spades five times in a row at bridge. Big business and big labor are firmly entrenched institutions and, barring a nuclear Armageddon, are here to stay.

Until this is admitted, economic theory is in deadlock with the facts. Markets and monopolies—including oligopolies and trade unions—are two very different animals. Markets can be controlled by monetary and fiscal means. Monopolies and oligopolies do not respond to the same financial levers because their pricing mechanisms are basically inelastic.

In effect, we have two separate but interrelated economies, which we have been trying to regulate (to the extent that this is not a misnomer) as one. Until we treat them as different and unequal in power and find some new and acceptable twenty-first-century approach to living and coping with both oligopolies and organized labor, there is no chance of permanently reducing both inflation and unemployment to acceptable levels.

It is difficult to admit that after almost a century of tinkering with antitrust laws, with numerous attempts to plug obvious loopholes, we are left with a more rigid economy than at the outset. The fact is repulsive to all true liberals. To even suggest a whole new approach to trusts, including the idea that sometimes they act in a manner that is not prejudicial to the public interest, is scandal itself.

Still, anyone who really cares about the poor and the unemployed must remove his or her head from the sand. All main-line economic theories are hopeless because they perpetuate the tradeoff between inflation and unemployment. All main-line theories are immoral because both inflation and involuntary unemployment are immoral. If jobs for all, with price stability, is the objective, a radical new approach is required.

NOTES

1 Richard E. Low, ed., *The Economics of Antitrust, Competition and Monopoly* (Englewood Cliffs, N.J.: Prentice-Hall, Inc., 1968). Donald Dewey, p. 62.

2 *Ibid*. Richard E. Low, p. 6.

3 ADAM SMITH, *Wealth of Nations* (London, England: Methuen and Co., 1964)l, Volume I, p. 130.

4 FREDERICK T. KNICKERBOCKER, *Oligopolistic Reaction and Multi-national Enterprise* (Boston, Mass.: Division of Research, Graduate School of Business Administration, Harvard University, 1973), pp. 6 – 7.

5 RICHARD HOFSTADTER, *The Age of Reform* (Northampton, England: John Dickens and Conner Ltd., 1962), p. 243.

6 *Regina v. Atlantic Sugar Refineries Co. Ltd., et al.* (Redpath

Industries Limited, St. Lawrence Sugar Limited, and S.L.S.R. Holdings Limited).

7 Annual Report of the Council of Economic Advisers, Washington, D.C., January 1981, p. 100.

8 Annual Report of the Council of Economic Advisers, February 1983, pp. 96 – 123.

9 *New York Times*, March 20, 1983, p. 22F.

10 MILTON and ROSE FRIEDMAN, *Free to Choose* (New York: Avon Books, 1980), p. 215.

11 *Maclean's*, June 13, 1983, p. 9.

12 LESTER C. THUROW, *Dangerous Currents* (New York: Random House, 1983), pp. 58 – 59.

13 *Ibid.*, p. 232.

10

The Freeze

Common sense dictates that the wage-price spiral must be stopped. The extended money squeeze of the 1975 – 82 period finally slowed it down considerably; but now that the monetary authorities have relaxed their restraint, there are ominous signs that the pace will soon quicken once more. Any effective policy must stop the spiral cold. Wages have to be brought back into line with productivity as they were in the golden post-Korean war years. There is no other way that the economy can be reflated and brought to a state of full employment and optimum output without fear of renewed inflation.

To accomplish this elusive goal I propose a two-stage solution. First, a twelve-month total freeze of wages and prices to unwind the spiral until inflation approaches zero. Second, a common-sense incomes policy to prevent big labor and big business from dancing the twist all over again.

This is not a plea for comprehensive wage and price controls. That point must be underlined because in an earlier book on the same subject several congressmen and members of Parliament stopped reading as soon as they saw the words. Their minds were so conditioned by their image of controls that they were closed to the possibility of a fresh approach. My plan is unique in the selectivity of its targets. It should not be confused with previous experiments because there are no precedents.

This applies to Stage Two, of course, because the idea of a wage-price freeze is far from new. It is a recognized policy option favored by many economists for use in an emergency. Douglas Peters, when he was Chief Economist for the Toronto Dominion Bank, told an October 1982 Conference Board of Canada business-outlook conference that "Canada should consider, as an initial program, a wage freeze for a period of up to 12 months."[1] The purpose is to wind inflation out of the system and permit a fresh start.

That is what I propose: a general freeze in which the only excepted items would be internationally traded commodities such as oil, copper, sugar, wheat, coffee, et cetera; also raw food products at the farm gate and fresh seafood at the dock. Experience has shown that these products cannot be effectively controlled.

The twelve-month duration is longer than usually proposed. This is dictated by the way we measure and report inflation. Although prices would cease to rise the day the policy took effect, the consumer price index for the previous twelve months would still register an increase. This should decline inexorably from its initial rate each month until it approaches zero when the year is up.

It is logical to wonder how inflation can be virtually eliminated in a year if commodities are excepted and the prices of some might well be expected to rise. In fact, any increases from this source should be more than offset by reductions in the cost of housing, manufactured goods, and bank interest that I will return to later.

Another question always arises as to why both wages and prices should be frozen. Many businessmen and some economists think it would be enough just to freeze wages. Once labor unit costs ceased to rise, prices could be kept in line by the simple expedient of not reflating too quickly. Soft markets would be a sufficient damper on prices. And in the case of oligopolies, as J. K. Galbraith has pointed out, they would probably be content not to raise prices but rather to increase their profits by concentrating on growth and expansion.[2]

The evidence of oligopolistic restraint is not totally convincing. But even assuming that the majority of the corporate giants would refrain from being greedy, in the world of political economy it is quite unreasonable to expect mandatory wage compliance without mandatory price compliance.

On the other hand, some of my union friends, as well as the Catholic Bishops, urge controls on prices but not wages. They base their argument on the fact that in recent years wages haven't kept pace with inflation. Real wages have fallen. It is true that there have been years when prices have outstripped wages, but that has not been the case over the long term. The graphs in Chapter 5 show that wages in the 1960s took off first and that prices then zoomed along behind in a blistering chase to absorb ever-increasing labor unit costs. Across the extended time frame, wages are still well ahead.

Furthermore, the concept of a general labor catch-up is illusory in an inflationary environment. Everyone knows what happens to a dog trying to catch its tail. This year's catch-up is next year's inflation. It is a self-perpetuating cycle that will never stop until it is attacked on two fronts. That means a freeze on wages as well as prices.

If a general freeze were planned and executed with reasonable care, prices should stabilize at once. Those provisions in all labor union contracts respecting future wage increases would have to be invalidated by statute. And all future price increases posted by manufacturers, wholesalers, and retailers would have to be rescinded. The object is a deep freeze, not just a light frost.

It is only natural that some exception has been taken to the retroactive feature of setting aside the financial provisions of outstanding collective agreements. It has been suggested that it might be a lot easier to get the cooperation of business and labor if, instead of the shock treatment I am recommending, the freeze only applied to new collective agreements in a more gradual approach.

It's a tempting idea because it might be easier to get cooperation and it would avoid the controversial element of retroactivity. But, in my opinion, it wouldn't work. The alternative would fail on grounds of both equity and matching expectations with results.

There are too many collective agreements in existence providing for substantial increases for periods up to four years; and many of these contain cost-of-living adjustment clauses. If those increases were allowed, while at the same time workers whose contracts expired about the time the plan was being implemented had their wages frozen, chaos would ensue. Grotesque distortions would develop that would make existing inequalities look like anthills. There would soon be a loud clamor for redress.

Even worse, from the standpoint of achieving the goal of price stability, would be the disastrous effect on expectations. It would be impossible to freeze prices in cases where wages and labor unit costs were still rising as a result of existing agreements. So prices in these special cases would continue to rise and it would be years before there was any hope of achieving true price stability. Workers whose wages had been frozen would feel they had been robbed. Their skepticism would raise serious doubts about the hope of eventual success and create pressure for the experiment to be abandoned. In that case the whole idea could be aborted in a sea of frustration.

It would be far better to bring all the runners back to the starting line. It may be rough justice but much fairer than permitting a privileged minority to ignore the starting gun. As far as the actual alteration in existing contracts is concerned, this would be more imaginary than real. What is the difference between a 6 or 5 percent raise with 6 or 5 percent inflation and no raise with zero inflation? In fact, most workers would be better off. Their settlements have not been keeping pace with inflation, so real wages have been falling. Consequently, when it comes to the bottom line of purchasing power, only a handful would be worse off, while the majority would gain substantially.

The idea of freezing prices for as long as twelve months raises hackles in business quarters. But in this area, too, the opposition is more in the nature of a conditioned reflex than a reasoned response. There are few areas of genuine concern. With rare exceptions, prices in effect at the time of the freeze would reflect current costs and consequently there should be few problems for the duration. The cost of labor—the biggest direct and indirect cost—would be frozen, and most material components would fall into the same category. Neither manufacturing nor service industries would have cause to fear.

While raw commodity prices would not be controlled, it is doubtful there would be substantial price increases until world demand had firmed considerably. To offset any increased cost of raw materials that did occur there would be lower financing costs resulting from lower interest rates, and enhanced productivity resulting from increased demand and higher capacity utilization.

Importers might feel a bit of a pinch if their foreign suppliers allowed their costs and prices to rise. But any increase in laid-down price would again be offset in part or in whole by the reduced cost of financing inventory and lower-than-anticipated domestic labor costs. Beyond that I doubt if it would upset most people if profit margins on imported cars and electronics were squeezed temporarily.

Exporters would be generally better off. To the extent that domestic costs rose less quickly than those of other countries, their competitive advantage would be enhanced. The immediate gain would far outstrip the disadvantage due to any modest hardening of the dollar.

For the economy as a whole there is always the possibility that a disastrous crop failure or some unexpected increase in the unregulated sector would exert upward pressure on consumer prices. Still, it is highly unlikely that the effect would be sufficient to prevent the CPI from approaching zero within the prescribed period.

The ace in the hole for true price stability is lower prices for manufactured goods. And there is no reason why this shouldn't happen. Once the upward pressure on unit costs due to the previous year's wage increases has been offset by productivity gains, prices of manufactured goods should begin to decline. Those in effect at the time the freeze is imposed should be considered maximums and not mini-mums. Long before the year has expired, the prices of a vast range of products—such as automobiles, bicycles, household appliances, and other manufactures—should begin to come down as labor unit costs in those industries actually decline. The effect on the CPI would be dramatic and should more than offset any increases in food and so forth.

Lower prices have been such a rare phenomenon for so long, however, that it might require a little "moral suasion" from someone as tough as the late C. D. Howe to break the psychological barriers. But break they must, because there is no way that price stability can be achieved unless the benefit of lower labor unit costs in capital-intensive industry is passed on to the consuming public through lower prices.

The great advantage of the freeze is the immediate effect on expectations. The instant stabilization of prices would have a profound psychological effect and it is reasonable to assume that behavior would begin to change with changing expectations. Interest rates would continue to drift down toward traditional single-digit levels and monetary authori-ties could accommodate sustained growth without fear of renewed inflation. Investors could settle for much lower interest rates—with zero inflation—and still have a higher real "after-tax, after-inflation" return left in their pockets.

Lower interest rates reduce the cost of all types of hous-ing and this, too, would exert a strong downward pressure on the CPI. The industry would flourish and people who hadn't been able to buy houses would be back in the market. Hopes would soon be raised and a general mood of optimism and movement would prevail.

The significance of this aspect of change was noted by

Paul McCracken and a group of eight independent experts in a report to the Secretary-General of the O.E.C.D.: "We recognize that in certain extremely difficult circumstances, resort to a wage stop and/or price freeze on a voluntary or statutory basis may be justified as an emergency measure, so long as it is accompanied by appropriate demand management policies.... The primary objective should be to cut into the price/wage spiral and provide the focal point for a significant wind-down of inflationary expectations."[3]

McCracken and his associates went on to record the obvious pitfalls: "Anticipation that controls are going to be introduced may accelerate inflation at the worst possible moment; the existence of controls may tempt governments to pursue unduly lax demand policies at a time of strong inflationary demand pressure, and the removal of controls is nearly always followed by a burst of price and wage increases as suppressed bargaining strength and market forces reassert themselves." They admit, however, "evidence from some countries shows that such programmes, if well-conceived and executed, can have a substantial short-term impact."[4]

Indeed! The results would be dramatic and as advertised. Provided, of course, that the program was statutory and applied equally to wages and prices. Voluntary plans are useless, and excluding either wages or prices would be subversive of the purpose. It's better to be all or nothing at all.

Dr. McCracken and his group of experts are right when they say it would be important not to give advance notice so that prices could be raised in anticipation. Should that happen, despite the precaution, it would be necessary to roll back prices to those that existed before the "defensive" pricing action began. And they are equally wise when they point out that any plan must be accompanied by appropriate demand-management policies. The monetary authorities would have to allow the economy to breathe while at the same time keeping the brakes on the printing presses. There is little point in arresting cost-push inflation just to replace it with the more traditional excess-demand variety.

Finally, it is true that the benefits would only be short-term if post-freeze conditions were as irrational as those that preceded it. But there is no reason why the mistakes of the past should be repeated indefinitely. The trauma of introducing a general freeze is only worthwhile as a step toward permanent rather than temporary price stability. To this end a "post-operative" stage is discussed in a subsequent chapter.

Admittedly, there are technical problems involved in a general freeze. Rules are required for new entrants to the labor force, including immigrants. Provision must also be made for the introduction of new products. But the necessary regulations could be kept simple and straightforward in view of their short duration. The consequences of any defects would be penny-ante in the over-all scheme of things.

Far more difficult is persuading politicians and potentates that the co-existence of negligible inflation and full employment is not an idle dream. At an Ottawa luncheon for a small group of reporters Finance Minister Marc Lalonde gave his "realistic" assessment of future prospects. "I don't think we should give up the goal of full employment," he said, but if he were able to bring unemployment down to 7 or 8 per cent by 1987, "I would be considered a hero."[5]

Lalonde's colleague, Transport Minister Lloyd Axworthy, is even more pessimistic. He has spoken of the need to "change the paradigm"—to alter our view of employment because of changed conditions. He suggests that jobs can no longer be defined as forty-hour work weeks, and that people engaged in training and education be counted among those with employment.⁶ Axworthy and Lalonde are not conditioned to believe in miracles, so they will have to be convinced.

The impossible dream is to persuade the big seven industrial countries—Canada, France, West Germany, Italy, Japan, the United Kingdom, and the United States—to undertake the introduction of such a policy simultaneously. A joint decision that would permit a sustained recovery of Western economies would be a sparkling contrast to the rhetorical minuets that have sometimes characterized the summit meetings of the seven leaders.

Following a joint declaration, a common starting date could be set, allowing only sufficient time for the preparation of the necessary legislation. Meanwhile the participation of other countries could be solicited. All would benefit from joint action. And harking back to Winston Churchill's metaphor, the ships of state, now buffeted by the wind and waves of economic uncertainty and upheaval, would stabilize and steam toward calm seas in convoy. That way any residual effects from imported inflation would be minimized.

Alas, the universal acceptance of such a "radical" approach is not likely until someone shows the way.⁷ Mimics abound but pioneers are rare.

Although any industrialized country could achieve dramatic results on its own initiative, there is little doubt that the United States would be the most logical choice. In size its economy is still number one, and major improvement in its performance tends to spill over on other economies, Canada's in particular.

Not only is the United States the most important place for economic reform to begin, but the chance of success is greater than in some other countries. For one thing, American labor is reasonably responsible. With some exceptions, it is primarily pragmatic and common-sense oriented—less "ideological" than many of its European counterparts.

"Ideology is baloney," the late George Meany once said. "There can be no ideological difference among real trade unionists."[8] In later years he even wondered out loud if strikes might not have outlived their usefulness and become too costly. It was not surprising, then, that the AFL – CIO under his leadership went so far as to propose a system of comprehensive controls as an alternative to Jimmy Carter's vague and ineffectual voluntary guidelines.

The degree of cooperation between management and labor during the economic crisis of 1981 – 82 was quite remarkable. It has been so good that it has virtually foreclosed serious consideration of new ideas for now. Monetarists can point to the 2.4 percent price rise from July '82 to July '83—the lowest in seventeen years—as a monumental victory. It is seen as justification for requesting further public patience concerning results on the employment front.

At a time when the U.S. economy is growing rapidly, and a group of 250 business economists predict unemployment to drop to 9.2 percent by the final quarter of 1983 and the Consumer Price Index to increase only 4.2 percent in the second half compared with the 4.9 percent expected earlier, it is extremely difficult to get people to worry about what will happen a few years down the road when settlements rise and the Fed is tempted to put on the brakes again.[9] As was the case in Canada years ago when the seeds of the crisis were being sown, the time is not propitious for serious discussion south of the border.

Canada's situation is different. Our performance has

been so much worse than in the United States that there is keen interest in new approaches. We have to do something new and different to catch up with our American neighbors. Our unemployment situation is even more desperate than theirs. Also, our inflation rate is still significantly higher, which makes our interest rates vulnerable to every cough and sneeze from the elephant. Canada has a powerful imperative to lead the way both for economic reasons and to enhance our self-esteem as a nation.

It is the responsibility of the federal government to act while seeking the cooperation of the provinces. It should be freely given, considering the economy and unemployment were so high on the agenda of the premiers powwow in Toronto last August (1983). They have nothing to lose and much to gain from a strong economy and the additional revenues it would produce.

One would expect the Supreme Court of Canada to uphold the validity of the initial legislation essential to the revitalization of the system and to the hopes and aspirations of millions of citizens. Certainly the sequence of double-digit inflation, a monetary crisis approaching the brink of disaster, and then double-digit unemployment constitutes a sufficient emergency to justify extraordinary action. In the unlikely event that the Court took a different view, a similar result could be achieved by means of legislation passed by the provincial legislatures. In the most unlikely event that Ottawa was stymied in both directions, a comparable program could be implemented by means of tax laws. The mechanics would be somewhat more cumbersome but nevertheless workable.

The Canadian political climate augurs well for the launch of bold new initiatives. Still, the simple expedient outlined in this chapter may sound pretty drastic—more like the kind of measure you would expect and put up with in time of war. But this is war—a war to preserve and revitalize the most productive and innovative economic system in the history of mankind.

NOTES

1 *Globe and Mail*, Toronto, October 8, 1982, p. B3.
2 JOHN KENNETH GALBRAITH, *The New Industrial State* (London: Hamish Hamilton Ltd., 1967), ch. XVIII.
3 Paul McCracken and a group of independent experts, *Towards Full Employment and Price Stability*. The Organization for Economic Co-operation and Development, 1977, pp. 218 – 19.
4 *Ibid.*, p. 219.
5 *Toronto Sun*, April 22, 1983, p. 3.
6 *Globe and Mail*, Toronto, July 23, 1983 p. B1.
7 Radical in the sense of seeking solutions based on first principles.
8 *The New American*, January 11, 1980, p. 7a.
9 *Toronto Star*, August 23, 1983, p. C3.

11

Jobs for All

It has long been the conventional wisdom that we must choose between fighting inflation and combatting unemployment. The price of a little success on one front is a somewhat greater disaster on the other, as we have just seen. Consequently, politicians and their advisers have tried to find the balance of misery most suitable to the economic, political, and social pressures of the time.

The concept of a tradeoff between inflation and unemployment was formalized by Professor A.W. Phillips, who plotted the relationship between the two on a curve that now bears his name.[1] It shows that as you move to reduce unemployment, prices and wages creep up. Some economists interpreted this discovery as economic law, but Paul Samuelson put its value in perspective: "The Phillips curve is a dramatic way of describing the dilemma for macro policy, even though it does not go beyond description to give us 'Explanation'."[2]

The Phillips curve doesn't provide an explanation because it is little more than a visual record of the consequences of an inconsistent and erratic monetary policy. The curve plots the gyrations between periods of tight money and easy money in much the same way that radar tracks an airplane wandering off course, first on one side of its intended flight path and then the other.

The usefulness of the curve and the validity of the trade-off theory has been subject to increasing question with the advent of stagflation, in which high prices and high unemployment occur simultaneously. In his search for an explanation of what might have gone wrong in the tradeoff theory, Samuelson takes refuge in the expectations hypothesis. Thus the fact that President Kennedy was able to engineer a long period of growth in the 1960s, before prices and wages began to behave badly, may have been exceptionally good luck. He was cashing in on Eisenhower's "investment in sadism"—a slack economy for many years in the '50s that may have killed off inflationary expectations and slowed down wage demands.[3] By the same reasoning, Samuelson suggested that it might take "years of economic retardation, as in the early 1970s. . . before inflationary momentum is overcome."[4]

That was a masterpiece of understatement. The years of retardation required were more prolonged and far more severe than those of the early 1970s. So much kinetic energy was lost by 1982 that concern began to shift from the residual inflationary momentum to fear of a possible collapse of the international monetary system.

Meanwhile the damage to the domestic economy has been incalculable. The loss of output from years of wasted capacity can be counted in the trillions of dollars. Far worse, the social consequences of jobs lost defy description. In January 1978 the Council of Economic Advisers estimated that it would take at least six years of 6.5 percent unemployment to reduce the inflation rate from 6 to 3 percent. "To achieve the same result in less time would require even higher unemployment rates."[5]

The thought was abhorrent at the time, and the realization has been bloodcurdling. The six years will soon be up, and while the inflation rate could be within 1 percent of the target in January '84—which would still be high compared to the golden years of the '50s—the level of unemployment required to achieve it was more than 50 percent greater than forecast "with over 12 million persons counted as unemployed" in December '82.[6] Additional millions were not accounted for in the figures because they had either taken part-time work or given up hope of finding employment and removed themselves, temporarily at least, from the work force. So even the gloomy predictions of Paul Samuelson and the Council of Economic Advisers appear to have been unduly optimistic.

Their error has been in putting too much stock in the theory of "expectations" and paying too little heed to the liaison between wages and prices. They have underestimated the upward momentum built into the system by collective agreements and cost-of-living adjustment clauses. In brief, too much adherence to the myth of the market and too little appreciation of the inertial cost-push of a schizo economy.

If it is axiomatic that full employment with stable prices is only possible in the long run if average wage increases equate with average productivity increases, then there are, in theory, only three ways of accomplishing the goal: monetary restraint, voluntary restraint, or legislative restraint.

Suppressing wages by monetary means has proven to be

too sadistic and too dangerous. The human costs are intolerable and the economic costs incalculable. As a cure for inflation it is far worse than the disease. The latest and most vigorous application had to be abandoned when it brought Western economies to the brink of disaster. Had it been pursued to its logical conclusion, the experiment would have created a world depression equal to or worse than that of the 1930s and with it an open invitation to establish alternative forms of government of either the totalitarian left or the totalitarian right.

Voluntarism is theoretically possible but patently unrealistic. Everyone is afraid to comply for fear his or her neighbor won't and he or she will never catch up. Besides, trade union leaders are politicians and their tactics in getting elected include promising more. It is totally unreasonable to expect restraint from those who enjoy unregulated power and have an incentive to use it.

The third option is the shock treatment I am proposing. It has the merit of being the only alternative that is genuinely in tune with economic reality. And isn't it better to undergo treatment capable of curing the fever rather than to remain a chronic invalid?

Once the freeze is in effect, fear of renewed inflation would subside. Notwithstanding Professor Phillips's perverse curve and the widely held belief that solutions to the inflation and unemployment problems are mutually exclusive, the Consumer Price Index would still be coming down as employment rose. The two problems would be resolved in tandem.

I am not suggesting that the money stock be increased at

rates comparable to those of the 1970s. Heaven forbid! Demand inflation remains an incipient threat and the whole point of the freeze is to stabilize costs and prices so that the economy can breathe and grow without the necessity of excessive monetary expansion.

Prior to the economic crisis of 1980 – 82 there was little doubt about government's ability to create the purchasing power to pursue full employment policies. As I stated at the outset, the techniques of demand management were not well understood in the nineteenth and early twentieth centuries— hence the periodic recessions and depressions that gave birth to the business cycle. But in the post – World War II years these were well understood: macroeconomics had come a long way since before the age of Keynes.

John Kennedy's experience in the 1960s is illustrative. By cutting taxes and providing incentives he increased the market for a wide range of goods and services, with multiplier effects throughout the whole economy. It was a winning technique that found an accepted place in all the textbooks.

Today, however, confidence in the ability of governments to achieve full employment has been lost. Respected economists, who are forecasting high rates of unemployment for years or decades to come, paint a totally gloomy and depressing picture for job-seekers. Their pessimism is usually linked to the specter of technological change. The American automobile industry is less competitive than the Japanese because it employs too many men and too few robots. To become competitive, more men will have to be displaced by machines. The advent of microchip technology is even more frightening. Tens of thousands of office workers will become redundant as "thinking machines" take over their jobs. The revolution in office procedures boggles the mind and bodes evil for the army of stenographers and clerks who know no other skills.

This bizarre portrait of a work world dominated by unfeeling machines and space-age robots is just an economic red herring, an excuse that monetarists and classical economists use to rationalize the failure of their theories. The technological scare acts as a cloak under which they can hide the inadequacies of their prescriptions.

The magnitude of the change that lies ahead must not be underrated. But it has to be put into perspective. How many harness-makers or carriage-makers are there among your acquaintances? How many sailing-ship masters do you know? The technological revolution hasn't just begun; it's been in progress for a long time. And as much as we resist or resent change, the human species is quite capable of adapting. The real problem is maintaining an economic environment that facilitates change—a situation in which an exciting new job appears when an old one hits the dust.

The unease that economists feel and express is not really related to the transition from automobiles to flying belts or from airplanes to space ships. It's not the long-run evolution that keeps them awake at night. It is their lack of any realistic plan to minimize the disruption caused by technological change. In brief, they no longer know how to maintain full employment because they have no formula for keeping wage settlements in line with productivity, and consequently no way of getting interest rates down to the levels existing in the golden years. They fear, and with just cause, that if they pursue full employment *under their rules*, prices and interest rates will begin to rise again and that the whole macabre exercise of curbing inflation temporarily will be exposed as a gigantic fraud.

One of the key ingredients of success in the early '60s that is missing from the current scenario is confidence. Sylvia Ostry, former chief economist of the Paris-based Organization for Economic Cooperation and Development, told an August '83 luncheon meeting of the American Statistical Association that the modest recovery expected over the next eighteen months, while welcome, can only be the beginning of the long road back to world economic health. "It would be most unwise to suggest that we're home free quite yet," she said.[7]

This view is widely shared by Canadian business and labor leaders. Like the economists, they think the number-one hurdle is high interest rates. "The recovery is at a stage where it could be aborted but probably it will continue at a much slower rate," says Sam Hughes, President of the 140,000-member Canadian Chamber of Commerce. "Hughes feels continuing high interest rates will cause Canadians to continue to save rather than buy and will not encourage the amount of investment that is needed to turn the present consumer-led recovery into a return to good times."[8]

Dennis McDermott, President of the two-million-strong Canadian Labour Congress, is even more emphatic. On October 2, 1983, he angrily accused Finance Minister Marc Lalonde of "political posturing" when he discounted the Conference Board of Canada's gloomy forecast. One more year of high interest rates will "strangle Canada's economy," he warned.[9]

McDermott's conviction is totally consistent with the CLC's campaign for lower interest rates as part of its recovery program. It is a position that has been vigorously and consistently supported by the *Toronto Star*. Editorially it has pointed out that real interest rates are at historic highs and that they must come down if the job market is to be expanded.

This raises the question of whether an independent interest rate policy for Canada is possible. We are told that it is impossible because any substantial deviation (downward) from U.S. rates would result in a massive outflow of capital and corresponding devaluation of the Canadian dollar. This is true as long as our inflation rate is as high as or higher than it is in the United States. Only with a lower inflation rate could we earn any flexibility. This fact was underlined by Allan MacEachen in his 1981 budget when he said that it was impossible for Canada to have an independent interest rate policy in the absence of an independent inflation policy.

Quite correct. This truism was underlined by Marc Lalonde in his response to Labor Department statistics showing that wage settlements in the second half of '82 were still high by historical standards. "We cannot keep on being competitive if we have wage settlements twice as high as the U.S. settlements. It is as simple as that."[10] As 1983 draws to a close we are still not competitive with the Americans. Until our performance is not only equal but superior to theirs, Canadian interest rates cannot be reduced substantially.

That is the reason that the freeze is so essential. Together with a plan for an incomes policy, it will change the expectations of both investors and consumers abruptly and profoundly. Both groups will be reassured that interest rates will fall and that wage-inspired inflation will not zoom off again. Of equal importance from the standpoint of achieving full employment, interest rates will fall to the point where they will stimulate investment and jobs in those areas where expansion can take place now—without waiting for the Buck Rogers era. Figure 8 illustrates the incredible impact of inflation and taxes on net yield to investors and underlines the extent to which interest rates might decline in the absence of inflation.

Lower interest rates will stimulate demand in the private, tax-producing sector, where it is needed most. The automobile industry is a case in point. Sales have turned up and the worst is over for car makers, thanks in part to much more favorable financial arrangements. Needless to say, the steel and farm implement industries, to name just two, could also use some additional orders!

Another big winner from lower interest rates, and any expansion in demand, would be the housing industry, which has had such a checkered career because of monetary extremes. This industry can increase output quickly, with ripple effects for appliances, furnishings, and equipment.

One other potential area of employment for both skilled and unskilled labor lies in the rehabilitation of existing buildings, both residential and commercial. A few municipalities have laws requiring owners to maintain their premises to an acceptable standard of health and safety or, failing that, to tear them down. Most jurisdictions, however, are much too indulgent. In a private-enterprise society, there is no reason why such laws should not be universally applied. Private owners are not allowed to drive automobiles in an unsafe condition. Why should owners of buildings expect to be treated differently? Certainly there is no reason why the state should be obliged to buy houses or other properties for sev-

Figure 8
Nominal, "Real," and Net After-tax Yields from Long-term U.S. Bonds

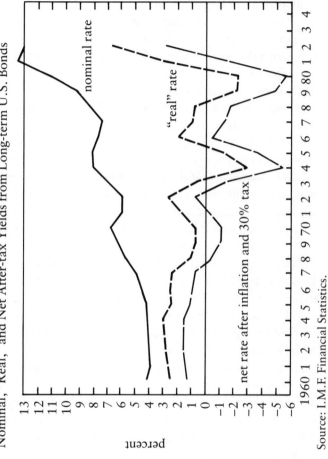

Source: I.M.F. Financial Statistics.

eral times their original cost as part of slum-clearance programs when the benefit of depreciation has already accrued
to individuals or corporations.

My point in mentioning these specifics is merely to
underline that there is no shortage of things to do. That puts
me in total disagreement with the conclusion reached by British writer Clive Jenkins in the book *Collapse of Work*, which
he co-authored.[11] After correctly noting that there are 25 million people in the Western industrialized world (now more
than 30 million) who are either unemployed or underemployed, he proceeds to the ridiculous myth that there is not
enough for everyone to do—the theory of "finite" demand.

Is he unaware that there are urban transit systems to be
designed and installed, polluted lakes and rivers to be cleaned
up, and new energy sources to be developed to reduce reliance of fossil fuels? If he were a Canadian, would he not care
that our beautiful lakes and forests are being contaminated
by "acid rain" from our own smokestacks and those of our
U.S. neighbors? Would he condone the incalculable damage
to our farms, forests, and tourist attractions?

The idea of finite work is bunk. We need more fuel-
efficient cars, planes, and houses. We need better hospitals
and chronic-care facilities for the old and mentally handi-
capped. And if our own insatiable appetite isn't enough, we
can show some genuine concern for the urgent needs of the
Third World. When millions of co-inhabitants of satellite
Earth lack pure water to drink, beds to sleep in, and enough
food to keep from starving, how can anyone say there's not
enough to do? There is virtually infinite potential demand.
The problem in meeting that demand lies in macroeconomic
policy!

A judicious blend of monetary and fiscal policies is important. In deciding where demand should be expanded, however, a neat balance should be maintained between the private and the public sectors. Expanding the public sector to the point where taxes discourage initiative can be self-defeating, as Augustus Caesar and many of his successors in authority have learned.

I am familiar with Professor Galbraith's thesis on "public squalor amidst private affluence," but as one who represented a working-class district in the Canadian Parliament for many years, I know that is only half the truth. It is much more precise, though less dramatic, to say "some public squalor (lack of parks and transportation facilities, et cetera) and some private squalor (slums, poverty) amidst some public affluence and some private affluence."[12]

People like those I represented in Parliament need better housing, private transportation, clothing, and adequate money for recreation and entertainment. They do not belong to any of the privileged classes and think differently and have a different set of personal and public priorities. They experience little joy from presenting their grievances in beautiful public buildings equipped with climate control and wall-to-wall broadloom.

Increases in effective demand should reflect the needs of all citizens, but especially those of the poor and the disadvantaged. This additional purchasing power should be expanded at a rate that will create job opportunities without going so far as to rekindle the fires of demand inflation.

I do not accept Milton Friedman's view that the annual increase in the money stock should be limited to some fixed static figure. It should be proportional to the increase in real

output. But the monetary authorities should have a little lee-
way to compensate for changes in the participation rate in the
work force or the kind of deflationary shock that occurred in
1974, when massive amounts of money flowed to the oil producers. They should also have the freedom to adjust for
changes in the velocity with which money changes hands, for
who could have foreseen the dramatic reduction in velocity
that occurred in 1982?

Although full employment is the target, it is doubtful
that the theoretically attractive unemployment rates of the
1940s and 1950s can be achieved. One obstacle is the phenomenon of ever-increasing "frictional unemployment," a
kind of voluntary unemployment that is a function of affluence. The wealthier that people become, the greater is the
temptation to take a short "sabbatical" between jobs. It can
be good for the soul to spend a few months reading books,
listening to music, or walking in the woods free from the
pressure of the marketplace.

In similar vein, an increasing number of students take
advantage of the hiatus between school graduation and their
first jobs to enjoy themselves and broaden their horizons
through travel. It's a luxury that increasing numbers can
afford. Their status, then, is deliberate and voluntary, and
because they are not actively seeking work, they are not really
"unemployed," although some of them, at least, have a way
of showing up in the statistics.

Another development that limits how far and how fast
we can reduce unemployment levels is the admitted increase
in structural unemployment. This is partly because of the
number of inadequately trained young people and women
entering the labor force and the mismatch between skills and

jobs. It also results from jobs moving from one place to another and workers being left behind. "Because transfer of human and physical resources is costly, and takes time, increased unemployment is a concomitant of structural change."[13]

Attitude is also part of the battle. In earlier decades, jobless craftsmen would have felt obliged to pack their bags and go where the jobs were, but recently there has been a progressive change in attitude. Artisans are often reluctant to take temporary work out of town, let alone move permanently. Unemployment insurance and other financial assistance has made it easy to say no.

The variation in wages is another factor. People line up for highly paid union and government jobs. Both provide plenty of perks, along with better-than-average security. Less interest is shown in the jobs with low pay. "For at least some people on the threshold of the labour market, the gap between what they can earn through gainful employment and that which they can obtain while not employed is just too small; the financial incentive to work has declined."[14]

There is no doubt that quite a few unemployed people don't really want to find work. At the same time I think that this reluctance has been overstated and that the great majority are willing to accept any reasonable offer. The work ethic is still strong with most people.

Mike Grbich is one of the casualties of stagflation who became one of Canada's working poor. "He's a 37 year-old laid-off steelworker who once earned $14 an hour but is now struggling to survive on minimum wage jobs that pay less than he could get if he were receiving welfare." As a minimum wage earner Grbich earned $606 a month, whereas on

welfare his family qualified for $714 general welfare assist-
ance in Metro Toronto.[15] The welfare check would have no
deductions for taxes, unemployment insurance, or the Canada Pension Plan. In addition, the family would receive free
OHIP, a drug card that pays for medicines, free eyeglasses,
free dental care for children, and free emergency dental care
for adults. But Grbich is proud and refuses to turn to welfare
for help.

One advantage of a well-managed economy would be
the ability to sort out who's who among the unemployed by
having enough jobs available for all willing takers. My definition of full employment is a situation in which the number of
people actively seeking work and the number of job openings
are roughly equal. Although the jobs and the applicants never
match perfectly, a person who isn't too fussy should be able to
obtain employment without undue delay. At the same time
there should still be sufficient slack that employers would not
ordinarily indulge in inflationary wage-bidding.

Where that line occurs is open to question. The program
I have outlined would soon answer the riddle.

NOTES

1 Formerly of the London School of Economics and the Australian
   National University.
2 PAUL A. SAMUELSON, *Economics*, 9th ed. (New York:
   McGraw-Hill Book Company, 1973), p. 833.
3 *Ibid*.
4 *Ibid*.

5 Annual Report of the Council of Economic Advisers, Washington, D.C., January 1978, p. 150.

6 Annual Report of the Council of Economic Advisers, February 1983, p. 29.

7 *Toronto Star*, August 17, 1983.

8 *Toronto Star*, October 3, 1983, p. A3.

9 *Ibid.*

10 *Toronto Star*, November 10, 1982, p. A3.

11 CLIVE JENKINS and BARRIE SHERMAN, *The Collapse of Work* (London: Eyre Methuen), 1979.

12 PAUL T. HELLYER, *Agenda: A Plan for Action* (Toronto: Prentice-Hall of Canada, 1971), p. 187.

13 Annual Report of the Council of Economic Advisers, February 1983, p. 39.

14 *Au courant*, Economic Council of Canada, Vol. 1, No. 1 (Spring 1980), p. 9.

15 *Toronto Star*, August 12, 1983, p. 1.

12

Incentive Indexing: An Incomes Policy for Monopolies and Oligopolies

Incentive indexing is the most appropriate way to describe my proposed incomes policy with its limited but essential objective. It is not to be mistaken for any system of comprehensive wage and price controls because it is not comparable. It is simply an antidote to the special immunities already granted to labor unions and a complement to antitrust laws that are quite impotent to cope with the peculiar characteristics of oligopolistic industry. It prescribes rules designed to prevent the abuse of power while at the same time encouraging both business and labor to enjoy the benefits of increased efficiency.

There is little point in submitting to a twelve-month wage and price freeze, then sitting idly by and watching the inflationary spiral begin afresh a few months later. The market power of big business and big unions, which gave rise to the problem, will not have disappeared in the interim. Consequently, some kind of incomes policy is necessary to act as a permanent "temperature control" to keep wages and prices from exploding.

Unfortunately, the record of success of incomes policies to date is not a happy one; thus many experts dismiss the idea

except for use in emergency situations. Still there are economists who seem to share my conviction that past failures are
attributable to a combination of careless design and inconsistent application rather than to the concept itself. Arthur
Burns, former Chairman of the Board of Governors of the
Federal Reserve System, once told me that governments will
continue to experiment with income policies. They will apply
them, then take them off again; try again and then backtrack,
until somebody, somewhere, eventually gets it right.

There have been a variety of experiments to date. In
Australia, for example, a master contract was negotiated
with one of the unions, usually the electrical union, and
referred to the courts for arbitration, if necessary; then all
succeeding contracts were settled on a basis of comparability.
The plan worked very well for many years until the mid-
1960s, when highly skilled labor in profitable industries
demanded and got raises greater than the standard. Whether
news of the big increases negotiated in Canada and the
United States sparked a wave of discontent, or the change of
heart resulted from other factors, the system broke down and
a philosophy of dog-eat-dog developed.

The Swedish approach was a little different. Following a
two-year wage "freeze" in the early '50s, the Swedish
Employers Confederation and the Confederation of Swedish
Trade Unions developed the practice of negotiating future
wage increases for manual workers. Two important aspects
were the attempt to arrange settlements for the greater part of
the Swedish economy, while at the same time attempting to
narrow the spread in pay differences between unions, and
then between groups within unions. This system, which was
voluntary, achieved considerable success, but began to break

down in the late '60s because of increased union militancy.

The postwar pioneer in direct government intervention, as opposed to Sweden's voluntary system, was Holland. Again, for a time, the Dutch policy of direct controls met with considerable success. But from the late '50s difficulties began to appear. A new Cabinet, with a slight bent to the right, was formed in 1959, and it placed greater emphasis on rewarding increased productivity within separate industries. Inevitably, pay increases in capital-intensive industries began to outpace those in less productive areas. Worker resentment grew as equity was lost and the lesson of "wage leadership" was ignored.

In Britain attempts to develop a voluntary system as an alternative to controls have centered on the concept of the social contract—an understanding between government and labor that wage increases be limited in the interests of society at large. Sometimes a carrot by way of tax incentives was offered, and sometimes not. The temporary success may have been sufficient to save the United Kingdom from economic disaster, but the fragile love affair between the former Callaghan government and its trade union supporters didn't last long. Poignant pleas to labor to settle for 5 percent gains fell on deaf ears.

Part of Callaghan's problem arose from mind-boggling settlements in the private sector. In 1978, following an eight-week strike, the Ford Motor Company in the United Kingdom granted its workers a 16.8 percent increase. Such settlements lift prices like kites in a stiff wind, and the Ford precedent gave the inflationary spiral a mighty twist. Naturally, everyone felt entitled to something comparable. Public-sector workers in particular decided to use their strategic leverage to crash the wage barrier, with disastrous results. The sick went unattended and garbage was piled mountain-high in downtown London. Public indignation became a powerful factor in the subsequent election of Margaret Thatcher's Conservatives.

Two Canadian attempts at incomes policies have ended unsatisfactorily. The first, in the spring of 1969, was the establishment of a Prices and Incomes Commission under the chairmanship of Dr. John Young. Its initial task was to solicit support of both labor and management for voluntary guidelines. At a National Conference on Price Stability in February 1970, management agreed to keep price increases below cost increases—i.e., to squeeze profits. After initial hesitation, however, labor refused to limit wage demands. Following a year and a half of fitful attempts, the commission meekly withdrew to the library—to do research. The last straw was the refusal of business to agree to a six-month extension of price restraint, a refusal stemming from labor's earlier intransigence.

The interesting epitaph to the death of the guidelines is that inflation was left alive and kicking. In his epilogue Dr. Young drew the following conclusion: "Without an early and substantial moderation of the size of wage and salary increases, and pricing policies which adequately reflect any moderation of cost increases. . . the choices will be renewed inflation, an unacceptable level of unemployment or compulsory measures of some kind."[1]

Before disbanding in the spring of 1972, the commission was asked to prepare a contingency plan for compulsory controls in case of emergency. A slightly modified version of the plan was introduced abruptly in the fall of 1975, just a year after the government ridiculed the necessity of controls in an election campaign. By then inflation had reached white-heat proportions, with individual wage settlements as high as 20 or 30 percent. Action was urgent and inescapable.

Unfortunately, the government hadn't learned from Dr. Young's admonition that "early and substantial moderation of the size of wage and salary increases" was imperative. Regulations limited wage settlements to 12 percent in 1976, with a 2 percent arithmetic reduction in each of the succeeding years. The rate of increase in unit costs began to level out and then subside slowly. Long before the excesses of 1974 and 1975 had been worked out of the system, however, controls were abandoned prematurely in 1978.

Allan MacEachen's widely publicized 6 and 5 percent restraint program hardly qualifies as a third attempt. In addition to being voluntary, except for public servants, it was more in the nature of a mopping-up operation than a new initiative. Wages and prices were predicted to fall because of the intensity of the recession and MacEachen was shrewd enough to get on the bandwagon. "If you look at the impact of 6 and 5 on the Consumer Price Index," observed Thomas Maxwell, Conference Board economist, "it's a very small component of it."[2]

That's not to say that it wasn't timely and well worth doing. One of its main achievements, in Maxwell's opinion, was to promote a feeling that "the government is at least trying to do something."[3] If it hadn't been for 6 and 5, public-service salaries would have been increasing at 10 – 12 percent compared to 0 – 6 in the private sector. That would have been a source of dissension and socially unacceptable. Also, with the program in place, some employers were able to use it as leverage in negotiations with their employees. Its over-all effect, however, was considerably less than advertised.

In the United States, the Annual Report of the President's Council of Economic Advisers set out criteria for both unions and management in 1962. The concept received general support for a few years, when it enjoyed a protective umbrella of civic responsibility. But by 1966 public discipline had pretty well evaporated, and whether the breakdown resulted from the Vietnam war or simply bigger wage demands is, in a sense, irrelevant. The lid on prices was effectively blown.

In August 1971 President Nixon confounded the experts by reversing his policy and introducing compulsory controls. Prices, incomes, and dividends were frozen for ninety days while spot checks were undertaken to ensure compliance. Phase Two was a period of tight controls following the freeze. Price stability during this period was encouraging—so much so, in fact, that Mr. Nixon moved on to Phase Three, which meant a return to voluntary controls. It didn't take long thereafter for conditions to return to "normal," with the whole plan being abandoned.

President Carter's October 1978 initiative launched "a program of price and pay standards designed to brake the price-wage spiral that has beset our economy for more than a decade."[4] His voluntary program included an explicit numerical ceiling for wage and fringe benefits, as well as a price deceleration standard for individual firms.

In January 1979 the President's Council underlined the difficulty with voluntary plans: "One of the obstacles to the success of voluntary wage and price standards is fear on the part of each group of workers that their observance of the wage standard could lead to a loss of real income if others do not cooperate, or if uncontrollable events, such as a serious crop shortage, result in price increases. Faced with such uncertainty and basing their price expectations on recent patterns of inflation, any workers might be reluctant to cooperate with the standards program. To improve the acceptability of the standards, the Administration is proposing to the Congress an innovative program of real wage insurance for those who observe them."[5]

Unfortunately, Congress did not pass the real wage insurance law as requested by the President. Furthermore, the courts rejected the legality of a system that lacked legislative authority.[6] So the guidelines remained voluntary in the literal sense.

"Studies by the Council of Economic Advisers reinforce the view that the President's program aided in keeping wage rates from accelerating. . . . However, both the employment cost index for union workers, and the effective wage change in collective bargaining units covering 1,000 workers or more, showed a greater increase in the 4 quarters through September 1979 than in the preceding 4 quarters."[7] At the same time productivity decreased and labor unit costs jumped by 11.3 percent, compared with 7 to 8 percent over the same four quarters a year earlier.[8]

No lesson from past experiences could be clearer than the observation that voluntary systems are essentially useless except for very brief periods at a time of acknowledged national crisis. To reinforce this conclusion, I have often asked audiences what their attitude would be if income tax was voluntary. Would they pay more, the same, or less tax than now required by law? Usually a couple of altruists insist

that they would pay the same; but the overwhelming majority admit honestly that they would remit considerably less if the amount were open to their discretion.

The principle is straightforward. Most people will obey laws that appear to be just if they are fairly enforced. But they will also take advantage of any concessions, opportunities, privileges, or even loopholes permitted by the law. In the words of that great nineteenth-century liberal John Stuart Mill, "the interference of law is required, not to overrule the judgement of individuals but to give effect to that judgement: they being unable to give effect to it except by concert, which concert again cannot be effectual unless it receives validity and sanction from the law."[9]

If an incomes policy must be mandatory to be effective, the next question that arises is whether or not it should apply to the whole economy. And, if not, what segments should be exempt?

The day that President Nixon's wage and price freeze was invoked in August 1971, I predicted that the controls would ultimately fail because they were attempting the impossible—never a sound foundation for economic policy. My objection was because of two factors: first, the inclusion of commodities, especially food; second, the simplistic treatment of the economy as one animal, without regard to the dichotomy between the market and oligopolistic sectors.[10]

Because I was raised on a farm and one of my first business ventures was marketing fruit, I was particularly sensitive on the first point. I recalled how quickly prices changed in response to supply and demand. Strawberries were an extreme case. A price set early in the season, when the berries first appeared, would be unrealistically high a week later.

Similarly, a price set in midseason would be far too low in early or late season, when supplies were scarce. The same problem applied to a lesser extent with other foods and many internationally traded commodities. While it is easy to pass regulations attempting to control prices in these cases, it is not easy to enforce them when they don't make sense in light of market conditions.

Just as it is impossible to effectively control the prices of commodities, which fluctuate with changing supply and demand, it is not necessary to impose controls where genuine market conditions exist. If it is theoretically possible for monetary policy to regulate prices in a free market economy, then it should be possible to regulate that part of the economy which is genuinely "free." One does not need to interfere with the market where the market actually governs.

The problem, as I explained earlier, is not the market. It is the fact that the "free" or market sector is frustrated in its operation by wage and price leadership from the sector that is, by definition, rigid. The economy is like two horses tied to the same wagon. The stronger horse—the one with market power—pulls out in front. So instead of a team, you have a lead horse getting out of line and tending to pull the wagon around in circles. A steady pull requires either an inflationary monetary policy, so that the laggard can keep up, or a tether on the lead horse.

The object of an essential incomes policy, then, is to control labor unit costs in the rigid sector and then to ensure that the benefits of increased productivity are shared by all members of society. Stated as a principle, the function of an incomes policy is to do the job that antitrust and anticombines laws were intended to do, have failed to do, and never can do. It is to keep the monopolies and oligopolies, the pow-

erful lead horse, in harness with the rest of the economy so that the whole can move forward together.

There is bound to be some difference of opinion as to who should be subject to regulation and who should not. Generally speaking, guidelines should apply to all monopolies, oligopolies, and cartels—all cases of "less than perfect" market conditions. This view has been expressed by others, including J.K. Galbraith, who has long promoted the concept.[11] Galbraith's list of oligopolistic industries includes automobiles, aluminum, rubber, synthetic fabric, transportation, tin cans, chewing gum, glass, soap, breakfast food, cigarettes, most electrical goods, aircraft, tractors, computers, typewriters, and most chemicals. One can nit-pick his selection, but it is indicative of the extent of the problem.

There will always be borderline cases where it is not entirely clear whether an industry is oligopolistic or not, so it should be possible for each company or industry to opt either for the free or the controlled sector. When a company or industry opts in favor of the regulated sector, it should have the protection of the law with regard to prices. That means that it would be exempt from anticombines law in respect of pricing, and that the public interest would be protected by observance of the profit guidelines laid down in the incomes policy.

When, on the other hand, a company or industry chooses in favor of the free and uncontrolled sector it must, in fact, compete in respect to prices as well as in other areas. Should there be any evidence of price fixing, identical bidding, or lack of genuine competition at any time, the choice should be subject to appeal. The public interest must be given the benefit of the doubt.

Official recognition of the existence and legitimacy of

oligopolies would not eliminate the necessity for public review of mergers and takeovers. But observance of guidelines set by an incomes policy should relieve officers and directors of companies from the threat of going to jail for doing what comes naturally.

On the labor side, all collective agreements should be assumed to be monopolistic in nature and subject to the policy. Of course there are cases where this is not literally true. Small unions have been broken and scab labor hired. But for all practical purposes the big unions do constitute a monopoly labor supply. Trying to differentiate between the big unions that do constitute a monopoly and the little ones that might not is too difficult and conducive to acrimony. So there is no simpler test, nor one easier to administer. A collective agreement, by definition, must be subject to the policy.

One final question remains. If big business and organized labour should be subject to an incomes policy, who should set the individual prices and wages? Looking for the answer takes us back to earlier experiments, including wartime experience. Nearly everyone who was then involved in controlling prices is against the reimposition of controls. But why? Controls did seem to work for awhile under emergency conditions when there was widespread public support for them. But later, anomalies appeared that led to black markets and other arrangements of convenience.

As always, the original prices had been those previously set by the trade. But as costs went up, and profit margins were squeezed, there was no quick, effective way to cope. Even when it was permissible for extra costs to be "passed through," the bureaucratic machinery was too cumbersome to avoid unacceptable delays. So businessmen adopted sur-

vival tactics of cutting quality, taking under-the-table payments, or removing the product from the market altogether.

Even when control prices are set by experts, the results are likely to be unsatisfactory. An example from my own experience in the housing business is illustrative. To encourage the production of houses to meet the desperate postwar shortage, the Canadian government had its agency, the Central (now Canada) Mortgage and Housing Corporation, insure high-ratio mortgage loans. For a builder to qualify, however, the CMHC retained the right to set the retail price of the house.

By the early '50s the market had eased to the point where, in many cases, the government's maximum price had become a convenient "minimum." Sellers confronted buyers with the fact that the asking price had been set by the government and in this way used the official figures to sustain prices higher than would have been set by the market. It was an inflexible system, however, so several builders consulted the responsible Minister about removing the controls. Inevitably, the reply from CMHC was always highly negative; price-setting would continue.

A builder myself, I volunteered to produce my company's cost sheets, which showed profit margins ranging from minus $400 to plus $1,900 a unit on the basis of the controlled prices.[12] Obviously, there was no incentive to build the unprofitable models, so purchasers were restricted in their choice. Bob Winters was impressed, and two weeks later the controls were removed. Within a month, new house prices in Toronto had fallen an average of $400 each.

In all the experiments with price controls and incomes policies to date, there is no case where a bureaucratic

machine has been able to set prices quickly enough and accurately enough to be acceptable. It is my opinion that a bureaucratic structure could never do so; its expertise is too limited and its data too stale. Governments simply should not get involved in the business of price-fixing. They should opt, instead, for mandatory profit guidelines, an alternative that eliminates the possibility of black-marketeering and of product substitution or restriction for the purpose of circumventing regulations.

Experience has shown the "order of magnitude" of the long-term return on capital associated with each industry. No single formula need apply. Guidelines could be devised that would accommodate the special requirements of different types of industries and conglomerates and still leave them the autonomy required for successful operation.

There would have to be a provision to allow profit-averaging over some reasonable period, say four years. It would be unfair, as well as unworkable, to require compliance in each calendar or fiscal year. Industry is faced with too many variables to alter course abruptly, and needs the flexibility to permit long-range planning.

Sensible guidelines would have no effect on investment. New, entrepreneurial companies would be exempt because they are invariably competitive. Guidelines would only apply to mature, oligopolistic industry, and in more than 90 percent of cases the allowable profit would be well in excess of anything companies have been able to achieve in recent years.

I have avoided specific figures because the purpose of this book is to discuss principles without getting bogged down in controversy over whether a specific industry should be allowed a 20 or 25 percent return on invested capital. But

in all cases the guidelines would be more than adequate to maintain investor interest.

To satisfy myself on this point I reviewed the profit results listed in Standard and Poor's 1982 list of 500 major companies and applied yardsticks that I thought would be considered fair and acceptable. Only four companies would have been affected that year—and then only if they had enjoyed equal profitability over a four-year period. Even then, compliance with the guidelines would have had such a marginal effect that I can't conceive of its influencing the attractiveness of the shares.

For the same reasons that government is not qualified to set individual prices, it should avoid getting involved in setting individual wages. The bureaucratic machinery required would bog down hopelessly. Not only that, it would just be a duplication of the existing facilities available to management and labor. So government should limit itself to the determination of an over-all wage guideline based on the previous year's increase in real output per member of the labor force adjusted to reflect any redistribution of income, either domestic or external, that might have to be taken into account.

Once the figure has been set, adjustments to individual wages and salaries should be made through direct management-labor channels. The only overriding criterion must be that the total package, including fringe benefits and wage drift[13]—a general job reclassification that results in higher average pay—does not exceed the limit set by the policy. This doesn't mean that no one would ever get an increase greater than the guideline. Privates would still be promoted to corporal, and corporals to sergeant. Assistant general

managers would become managers and earn the raise consistent with their increased responsibilities. This is all provided
for in the system. Only an attempt to accelerate the tempo of
promotion for the sole purpose of cheating on the guidelines
would destroy their effect and consequently would be
prohibited.

Although union wages would be indexed to average productivity increases, and this tractor-trailer relationship
should be sufficient incentive for everyone to pull together to
increase output, a powerful case can be made for allowing
profit-sharing agreements as an added bonus. I personally
would both permit and encourage collective agreements providing for a bonus to workers of up to 5 percent of company
profits—through either direct or deferred profit-sharing
plans.

This idea was promoted by the late Walter Reuther when
he was President of the United Auto Workers. It was not popular with management at the time, but as the years pass it is
being recognized as the type of concession whereby corporations have little to lose and much to gain. There is, after all,
nothing like a work force with a direct incentive to be
productive.

Workers would gain on both fronts. First directly, as
their company prospered, and then through higher wages as
better individual results contributed to a higher national average of increased efficiency. There would be a strong incentive
to establish joint management-labor productivity councils in
each bargaining unit because everyone would benefit from
the results of initiative and imagination. Improved performance in thousands of individual bargaining units would soon
add up to a measurable increase in the national guidelines.

One other point involves the internal redistribution of

income referred to earlier. It is inevitable, whenever a freeze occurs, that in some cases a group or class of workers would be caught at a disadvantage. This cannot be avoided, and the best that can be done is to establish a body to hear grievances and arbitrate claims for catch-up. This task might be assigned to a wage board appointed exclusively, or at least predominantly, from the ranks of trade unions. The board would hear and evaluate complaints and decide how much catch-up, if any, was justified and the time frame over which it would be allowed.

All awards of this kind would have to fit within the total sum provided by law and excluded from general distribution. In other words, the general guidelines would be a little bit less than the average increase in output for the previous year so that there would be a small pool available for the cases of catch-up—at least in the early years until the most blatant distortions had been ironed out.

Enforcement of all wage and profit guidelines would be effected by means of the income and corporations tax laws. A schedule of profit guidelines would be incorporated at the outset and amended only if experience proved that they were too restrictive. The wages guidelines would be amended each year to reflect the average productivity increase for the previous year.

Using the existing tax laws is the simplest and most efficient method of enforcement because the Internal Revenue System in the United States and Revenue Canada at home are well equipped for the task and no expensive new bureaucracy is required. Excess wage and profit increases would simply be taxed at 100 percent, with additional penalties for cases of deliberate non-compliance.

In Canada, a constitutional amendment giving Ottawa

jurisdiction over labor law would be highly desirable, if not essential to the long-term success of the system. It is totally incongruous for one level of government to have responsibility for money and banking while another has the principal say in respect of wage settlements that affect the demand for money so directly. What is required is a two-way exchange of power that would make the federal government directly accountable for the operation of the economy while transferring to the provinces some of those functions that can be filled with greater sensitivity at the provincial and municipal levels.

Until 1982 such an exchange, though theoretically desirable, would have been unthinkable in practical terms. But now that Pierre Trudeau and the premiers have succeeded in patriating a Canadian Constitution that is not subject to veto by any single province, a common-sense proposal of this nature is a realistic objective, especially in the context of the current economic malaise.

This is not the place to set out the specifics of either an incomes policy or constitutional arrangements. The staff work involved should be undertaken in partnership by government, management, and labor. Not only is any system more likely to be acceptable if it is developed in a spirit of cooperation, but early private sector involvement should guarantee the avoidance of many pitfalls. This is an added advantage of the twelve-month freeze: the provision of ample time for the preparation of thoughtful and meticulous regulations.

Even then, some minor flaws are to be expected. Arthur Burns would be likely to agree that the probability of developing a "perfect system" is too remote to be taken seriously.

Like Marx's long-awaited withering away of the state, the notion of an earthly Utopia will remain a will-o'-the-wisp as long as there are people involved. The most we can hope for is a system that avoids some of the grievous errors associated with previous experiments and embodies principles compatible with the real economic environment in which it would be applied.

I have tried to incorporate all the significant lessons from past experience into the design of a new system. Still, I am sure someone will wonder if I have considered the merits of alternate new ideas currently in vogue, such as the concept of a tax-based incomes policy (TIP). I have, and found them wanting.

The 1981 report of the President's Council of Economic Advisers discusses tax-based incomes policies at some length: "Several choices must be made in designing a TIP. First, should it dispense rewards or levy penalties? Second, should receiving the penalty or reward depend only on being above or below the standard (a 'hurdle' TIP), or should the size of the penalty or reward be graduated in accordance with the difference between the standard and the actual pay or price increase (a 'continuous' TIP)? Third, should the TIP apply to pay, to prices, or to both? These choices require striking a balance among equity, efficiency, administrative ease and effectiveness in reducing inflation."[14]

The Council concludes: "For several reasons, a reward pay TIP is probably preferable to a penalty pay TIP." This would cost a substantial amount in forgone revenues (tax credits), however, so "a reward TIP would only be feasible when tax cuts were being considered. . . . A TIP limited to a few thousand large firms with computerized personnel records would have much smaller public and private administrative costs than a TIP that included millions of small firms." But this "would be vigorously opposed by workers in small firms, who would argue, rightly, that they were being deprived of a potential tax cut."[15]

The final major issue, the Council suggests, is whether a TIP should be permanent or temporary. "The answer seems to be that a permanent TIP would not be feasible because of the distortions it would create by discouraging changes in relative wages. A TIP might introduce further distortions as people changed their behavior to circumvent the intent of the policy while remaining technically in compliance with the standard."[16]

"On balance," concluded the Council, "a temporary hurdle TIP—a tax credit to groups of workers whose average pay increase does not exceed a specified standard—seems superior to other variants." This would probably have to be coupled with a price TIP for political reasons "because restraints on pay alone, even with a reward TIP, might appear inequitable." The Council estimated that for a cost of $12 billion its temporary, voluntary system might reduce wage inflation by .79 to .93 percent, depending on the pay standard set. For $16 billion, an improvement of .91 to 1.09 percent might be expected.[17]

To impose such a complicated system for such a small benefit seems to me a little bit ridiculous. The plan fails to recognize either the permanent nature and influence of monopoly power or the likelihood that the wage spiral would resume its upward trend when the TIP was abandoned. A TIP, in my opinion, would be just another temporary expedient, which, like Jimmy Carter's voluntary scheme, might be better than nothing, but not much better.

It is axiomatic that stable prices are impossible without constant labor unit costs. Therefore it follows that inflation will exit permanently only with an incentive-indexed incomes policy that deals forcibly and realistically with the structural effects of monopoly power. To do this it must (a) be mandatory, (b) be permanent, (c) apply only to the rigid sector of the economy, and (d) allow companies and their unions to set their own prices and wages within the parameters set down by the policy.

NOTES

1 *Ottawa Citizen*, December 2, 1970.

2 *Toronto Star*, Sunday, July 3, 1983, p. 1.

3 *Ibid*.

4 Economic Report of the President, January 1979, p. 4.

5 Annual Report of the Council of Economic Advisers, Washington, D.C., January 1979, p. 82.

6 Decision by U.S. District Judge Barrington Parker, May 31, 1979.

7 Annual Report of the Council of Economic Advisers, January 1980, pp. 36 – 38.

8 *Ibid*.

9 *Principles of Political Economy*, edited with introduction by Sir William Ashley (New York: Augustus M. Kelly Publishers, 1909), p. 963.

10 The prediction was stated in a press release issued by Action Canada.

11 JOHN KENNETH GALBRAITH, *The New Industrial State* (Boston: Houghton Mifflin Co., 1971).

12 On a $15,000 house.

13 Wage drift is an arbitrary system of job reclassification that could nullify the intent of wage guidelines or controls.

14 Annual Report of the Council of Economic Advisers, January 1981, pp. 61 – 65.

15 *Ibid*.

16 *Ibid*.

17 *Ibid*.

13

Everybody Wins

Is my radical program possible? After more than a decade of talking to all kinds of people about the ideas and gauging their reactions, I am convinced that it is. The reason, in a nutshell, is that everybody wins, nobody loses. Once people understand that, opposition subsides and interest is keen. All that is required is bold political action backed by a first-class education campaign.

Heaven knows it wouldn't be easy. There would be stiff opposition from both business and labor. One can't expect an intellectual about-face without extended soul-searching. No one likes to exchange comfortable old shoes for tight-fitting new ones, and big business and big labor have had such a freewheeling good time with their free collective bargaining that they won't relish seeing the "right" limited by externally imposed discipline.

Unlike many observers, however, I have never believed that either big business or big labor is basically immoral. Both, being human, put self-interest first. But the great majority are just as conscientious in their citizenship as any other group; and they will find great difficulty in refuting the charge that the way they have been exercising their rights since the mid-1960s has resulted in sentencing millions of their fellow citizens to involuntary unemployment just as surely and directly as a judge sentences a felon to jail. No one has the right—either natural or acquired by legislation—to commit such an unforgivable crime.

When it comes to specific objections, the man on the street will have to be shown that real wages are quite independent of nominal wages and that his real purchasing power will rise faster in an economy featuring full employment and high productivity. The average working person is endowed with innate common sense, and in small groups I have encountered little resistance to the concept of an improved system. They are moved by the attraction of higher real wages but equally by the prospect of improved job security, or at least the opportunity to find a new job should the old one disappear.

Businessmen will probably be harder to convince. The "free enterprise" theology is deeply ingrained, and the kind of natural skepticism Porgy and Bess expressed about the story of Jonah and the whale has never entered their consciousness. Currently, the myth is being reinforced by the absolute certainty of young whiz kids graduating from the academy in one of its most conservative moods.

In fact most businessmen are ambivalent about government intervention in the marketplace. Pleas to limit the access of cars from Japan, shirts from Hong Kong, or shoes from Italy by means of quotas or duties are commonplace and welcome. Government-imposed standards to protect the purity of air and water are received with less enthusiasm.

Similarly, free-enterprise farmers show no compunction about accepting subsidies to grow, or not to grow, specific crops. And business generally is seldom if ever averse to government assistance in providing the infrastructure essential to the operation or expansion of their enterprise.

It is a fallacy to pretend that government can disconnect and leave the market totally to its own self-correcting mechanisms. Reality is far too complicated, and it is no longer a question of intervention or non-intervention but rather one of the quantity and quality of intervention.

Had governments, business, and academics understood monetary policy and the mechanics of exchange well enough to prevent business cycles in the two centuries following the Industrial Revolution, there might have been no need for collective bargaining. But they didn't and such bargaining is now a cherished part of Western culture. The system eventually went berserk, however, and now the government must restore socially acceptable behavior.

In addition to its programmed paranoia about intervention, business is concerned about an increase in the size of the federal bureaucracy. It is a legitimate concern, but a close examination of my proposal reveals good news on this front. As enforcement of the guidelines would be the responsibility of the taxation authorities, the only additional personnel required would be the members of the Labor Board and their staff—a mere drop in the ocean. Far more significant would be the reduction in bureaucracy made possible by an economy working consistently at or near capacity. Thousands of public servants now engaged in administering unemployment insurance and welfare would become redundant and available to test their skills in the tax-producing sector of the economy. The demand for a vast range of social services and social workers would diminish with the return and entrenchment of good times. On balance, the size of the bureaucracy could be reduced significantly without any dilution in the provision of essential services. Smaller numbers would mean a smaller deficit and ultimately a lesser tax burden when the system was operating at full force.

Academics would be every bit as difficult as businessmen to convince. Many of them are on the record that there is no "quick fix" for our moribund economy and that we should expect many years of modest inflation and unusually high unemployment. Indeed, Milton Friedman and others have already cautioned Chairman Volcker not to allow recovery at a pace that would result in renewed inflation. One suspects that part of the concern stems from the realization that an acceptable rate and level of recovery might re-create the kind of conditions we have just gone through torture to eliminate.

One objection I hear from economists is that permanent wage guidelines would distort the natural market allocation of labor. Excuse my raised eyebrow. Of course it would, but anyone who carefully examines the wild distortions created by free collective bargaining over the last fifteen years and is still unduly concerned about the effects of income guidelines must qualify for the award of "Modern Economic Nelson" for looking through the telescope with a blind eye.

There is no question that a pure market would allocate labor more efficiently than any kind of arbitrary guideline, no matter how good. A hamburger stand with a roaring business on one side of the street can attract workers from a moribund hotdog stand across the way by paying higher wages. Were it not for the intervention of union power, the same kind of adjustment would occur in big business if wages were determined exclusively by market conditions. But we haven't had that kind of market; we don't have and we won't have. So we have to make the best of what we've got.

Even with wage guidelines it is possible to influence the allocation of labor in a crisis or if the national interest demands. If, for example, there were a critical shortage of workers in the aircraft industry and a bigger output was clearly required in the national interest, a Congress or Parliament could direct the labor board to authorize a pay increase above the average and "charge" the extra increment to its discretionary or catch-up allotment. This should be a rare step, and never taken lightly. Nevertheless, anything is possible if the national interest dictates.

Politicians should be as easy as anyone to convince. They have a powerful driving motive to find and implement improvements to the economic system. If they don't, they run the risk of electoral defeat.

In the United Kingdom the partial collapse and seemingly hopeless drift of a once-great industrial economy has been relevant to the rise and fall of political fortunes. Successive governments have reaped the whirlwind of discontent, and Margaret Thatcher owes much of her initial success to the morass in which the Callaghan government found itself.

I had predicted that Margaret Thatcher's identification with monetarist sadism would lead to her political demise. Indeed, that appeared certain until the outbreak of the Falklands war. Her firm, unshakable stand in that conflict sensitized a latent patriotic nerve in British hearts and her popularity rebounded. Electors, cheered by her character and strong resolve, gave the lady an overwhelming new mandate. But it is still fair to say that, had it not been for the Falkland miracle, the 13-plus percent unemployment caused by monetary contraction might have proved politically fatal.

In Canada several governments have been defeated at least in part as a result of monetary policy. It was a factor in the eclipse of the St. Laurent government in 1957. And it played an even greater part in John Diefenbaker's two-stage defeat in 1962 and 1963. High unemployment, rising inflation, and the devaluation of the Canadian dollar to $92^{1}/_{2}$ cents—the "Diefenbuck"—all cost votes.

Economics was also an ingredient in Pierre Trudeau's close miss in 1972, and his temporary demise in 1979, as it was in Joe Clark's early execution a year later. People get sick of high prices, high unemployment, high taxes, high interest rates, and low hopes of improvement.

In the United States both Republicans and Democrats have reason to be concerned. Those questions that Ronald Reagan asked voters in November 1979 must still be ringing in his memory. Were they better off than they had been four years earlier? Had their lot improved? What answers will voters give when they are asked the same questions again? And have the Democrats benefited from being out of office? Have they used the time to advantage to develop any new plans that won't lead to renewed inflation and even greater deficits?

There is scant evidence that politicians learn from experience, but I profoundly hope that someone, somewhere, will take the long view. Once one or more countries take the plunge, the pressure on others to follow will be immense. To be first off the diving board, however, requires courage— courage backed by the conviction that some of our oft-repeated but elusive goals can be achieved, conviction born of concern that those goals must be achieved lest the current cynicism toward politics and politicians undermine faith in our most hallowed institutions.

The stakes are high, but politicians willing to take the risk would have a lot going for them. Conservatives would be pleased by the prospect of sound money. Liberals should be ecstatic to realize that at last they would be able to attack basic social problems from a firm and stable base. There are some high cards to play when it comes to selling the idea to voters—the cards that are absolutely essential to achieving the "non-inflationary, sustained growth" that President Reagan stated as his goal at the Williamsburg Summit Conference.

Incredible as it may seem, the policy changes I have proposed would benefit everyone—except the infinitesimal minority who prosper from other people's misfortune. The vast majority would benefit because the scheme includes no tradeoffs favoring one group at the expense of another. It's a legitimate game plan where everybody wins.

The two principal goals are full employment and stable prices. These are the bedrock foundation on which a sane and humane economic system can stand without fear of collapse. They provide the essential underpinning for increased output, higher productivity, bigger real wage gains, enhanced profits, lower interest rates, and fewer strikes.

It is difficult to choose between the two pillars because they are so closely related. Inflation is a form of larceny, so it must be fought on moral grounds. "To benefit anyone," admitted Bank of Canada Governor Bouey, "it must continue to take advantage of at least some people."[1] Eliminating inflation as a feature of economic life, therefore, would restore a sense of equity that is beyond the competence of our judicial system.

If I had to select one group of citizens who would benefit more than any other, however, it would have to be the unemployed. For someone who wants to work, there is nothing more degrading than involuntary idleness. To be constantly rebuffed can be soul-destroying, especially for those who come to believe that they themselves, rather than the system, are at fault.

My conscience has never allowed me to accept the callous notion that a few hundred thousand or a million extra unemployed is a small price to pay for monetary stability. Apart from the fact that the traditional money squeeze doesn't work as smoothly as advertised, the inevitable cost in loss of jobs is too big a sacrifice for the hapless individuals involved.

Although the unemployed would be among the biggest winners, they wouldn't be the only beneficiaries. The entire population would gain on many fronts. As employment increased, so would output. Instead of being a drain on the public purse, workers would be contributing to it. Then the worrisome budget deficit could be reduced.

In addition to the extra production from a higher level of employment, there would be a general increase in productivity. It's one of the myths of economics that people work harder when unemployment is high because they fear for their jobs. In fact, they featherbed more in times of high unemployment because they don't want to work themselves out of a job. Once jobs become more plentiful, everyone can afford to work a little harder.

Some underemployment results from deliberate corporate policy in periods of recession. Personnel are kept on staff in anticipation of an economic upturn because it is no more expensive and much more convenient than training new employees when the pressure is on. Naturally, the productivity of the underemployed rises sharply as the economy expands.

Another contribution to productivity would be an increase in capital investment. When inflation is rampant, prudent investors direct a proportion of their savings to the purchase of gold, silver, stamps, coins, and works of art. This may be wise as a means of protecting purchasing power, but it is the contemporary equivalent of the biblical steward burying his coin in the back yard. It is not a contribution toward the creation of wealth. Without inflation, there is less temptation to hoard. It makes much more sense to invest in new productive machinery, and this in turn increases productivity.

One additional factor of incalculable benefit would be the reduction in the number of strikes and lockouts. Although corporate executives commonly assume that lost net earnings represent the true cost of a strike, such figures fail to take account of a strike's other significant financial effects. Lost profits represent only the tip of the iceberg. In an article entitled "Strikes Cost More than You Think," Woodruff Imberman catalogues a long list of tangible and intangible costs: "When union leaders and the company begin to trade charges, workers usually retaliate by putting forth less effort and less care. Productivity declines about 2% to 12% in the three or four weeks preceding the strike. . . . During a strike, some employees drift away and never return. In such cases costly advertising, selection and training procedures are involved."[2] Imberman's list continues to include other costs ranging from legal fees to sabotage.

Ironically, it is labor that gains most from higher productivity and industrial peace. Because wages and salaries comprise about two-thirds of the national income, hourly and salaried employees would be the principal beneficiaries of increased output resulting from an improved system.

Nominal wage increases would, admittedly, be smaller. But as I have argued throughout this book, that is really irrelevant. It is the content by weight and not the size of the pay package that determines its purchasing power. It is in our own best interests as workers, therefore, to adopt a more relaxed attitude toward business in the knowledge that we will ultimately get the lion's share of any savings we are able to achieve for our employers. Profits are needed to finance the extra machinery, and more technologically advanced machinery, necessary to increase productivity.

By pursuing the practice of consultation and cooperation rather than confrontation between labor and management, real incomes could be expected to rise faster than in the last decade. In a well-managed economy—one that isn't gyrating between tight money and easy money and where work stoppages and slowdowns become increasingly rare as they are recognized to be self-defeating of workers' real interest—there is no reason why the average productivity rate shouldn't be much better than the dismal record of the 1975 – 82 period.

It must be pointed out, however, that we can have higher pay or shorter working hours but not both, except in moderation. Not long ago an economics professor—who should have known better—advocated an immediate reduction in the work week to thirty hours, with the same take-home pay. Had he checked the arithmetic he would have known that it requires at least ten years' total increase in productivity to affect the reduction without a loss in real pay.

Another entry in the competition for increased productivity is the goal of ensuring safer products and greater environmental protection. In the United States, the Reagan administration relaxed some of the requirements that were already on the books. Many conservationists think it went too far. On the other hand, overzealous officials and citizens groups in all countries must constantly bear in mind that this, too, is a tradeoff. As the President's Council pointed out: "Regulation is very costly; and benefits should be closely compared with costs in the design of regulatory legislation and specific regulations."[3]

Although labor would be a big winner in an improved system, this would not be at the expense of business, which would have its own stack of chips to cash. Business has always manned the ramparts when the word "guidelines" is mentioned. Yet a more thoughtful analysis will show that business can achieve some of its most coveted objectives, with predictability at the top of the list. Business can bid on goods or projects with confidence when it knows what its costs are likely to be. The escalator clauses that have strangled many worthwhile projects, both public and private, should die on the vine.

Meeting delivery schedules should be a lot easier, too, with a lower incidence of strikes. That institutional relic of the jungle age should become virtually extinct in relation to money issues and be reserved for cases of intolerable working conditions perpetuated by unfeeling nineteenth-century-type managers.

Although certainty of costs and the near elimination of strikes should provide a euphoric climate for harassed entrepreneurs, these advantages still can't substitute for the bottom line: profits. It is in this department that business has nothing to fear. All of the elements of profitability—predictable costs, a secure labor force, and an expanding, recession-free economy—would be present. The rest would be up to the managers themselves.

Even the oligopolies should do as well or better than ever. If it had been their practice to place greater emphasis on costs than on market conditions in setting prices, then the only new phenomenon resulting from the guidelines would be lower prices to reflect declining unit labor costs.

The biggest gain of all for many businesses would be the substitution of real for nominal profits. Inflation distorts the profits posted by business and makes them appear to be doing better than they really are. Corporate executives who have been conning their shareholders by describing profits of 5 or 6 percent as "satisfactory" should choke on their own deceit. Instead, they should have been saying that "by running hard we have just managed to break even—after inflation."

It is, after all, real profits that are needed to encourage savings and capital investment. It takes real profits, not just the recycling of shrinking paper, to finance expansion and new job opportunities. Business would be an early winner after the freeze was imposed and the pressure of cost increases was lifted. But this initial advantage would just be money in the bank for the whole system as it settled into a new and stable equilibrium.

One of the most compelling attractions of the improved system is lower interest rates. Everyone would benefit either directly or indirectly. Without inflation, the Bank of Canada and the central banks of other countries could lower their

rediscount rates and let interest rates settle to more traditional single-digit levels. Lower interest rates would have a
significant beneficial effect for utilities such as electricity and
telephone, where debt service charges are a substantial part
of total costs. Business in general would benefit by being able
to borrow more cheaply, and consumers would enjoy a similar advantage in financing household purchases.

It is in the housing field, however, that the most profound change would occur. The industry should flourish as
the cost of both home ownership and rental accommodation
dropped dramatically. With interest rates falling close to their
levels in the 1950s—about 5 percent—tens of thousands of
young people who have been effectively barred from home
ownership for almost a decade would have their freedom of
choice restored.

The figures are startling. In Metro Toronto a typical
$100,000 house in the suburbs qualifies for a Canada Mort-
gage and Housing Corporation insured maximum loan of
$89,320. With a 12 percent mortgage, amortized over
twenty-five years, the houses carries for $1,046 a month
principal, interest, and taxes, of which the lion's share is
interest. Purchasers need an income of $50,252 under the old
"25 percent of income for a roof over your head" rule. Anyone willing to stretch to 30 percent of income, the maximum
allowed, can qualify with $41,868.

The same house with the same mortgage, but at 5 percent interest, would carry for $644 a month. Buyers would
only need $30,936 income under the 25 percent rule, or
$25,780 if they went the limit.

A more modest $60,000 house in a smaller center can be
mortgaged for $54,810. At 12 percent the monthly carrying

charges are $640. Income requirements are $30,748 at 25 percent of income, ranging down to $25,623 at 30 percent. With a 5 percent mortgage, that house would carry for $393 a month. Newlyweds earning $18,902 could buy one with 25 percent of their income. Anyone willing to squeeze other purchases in order to get into a place of their own could do so with as little as $15,752 income.[4]

The improved system would have world-wide repercussions. The currency of any participating country would harden as soon as world markets were convinced of the seriousness of the plan. The rationale for further oil price increases, even when demand catches up with supply, would diminish because the real purchasing power of each barrel would no longer be eroded by inflation.

To the extent that the improved system spread across the Western world, as ultimately it must if capitalism is to survive and attract the allegiance of the next generation, the impact in both human and economic terms would be incalculable.

Most important, the performance of a great economic system would cease to be erratic and often unpredictable. Business cycles, as we have known them for generations, would end and the term would lose its place in the economic lexicon.

NOTES

1 Remarks to the annual meeting dinner of the Canadian Life Insurance Association, Ottawa, May 28, 1975.
2 *Harvard Business Review*, May – June 1979, pp. 133 – 38.

3 Annual Report of the Council of Economic Advisers, Washington, D.C., January 1979, p. 69.

4 Figures courtesy of the Royal Bank of Canada, Head Office, Montreal, June 1983.

14

The Liberal Agenda

At first blush it might seem that reaching the twin goals of
stable prices and full employment would produce an economic heaven on earth. No doubt the situation would be
heavenly compared to the present unholy mess. But these are
not ends in themselves; they are only means—the tools necessary for the emancipation of human life and the liberation of
the human spirit.

Canadian Liberals face many important issues for which
these tools are required. The list includes Medicare, pension
reform, housing, pollution control, energy self-sufficiency,
the elimination of poverty, among others. And in addition to
those domestic concerns, there is the morally compelling
requirement to help the people of the Third World develop
the means to a better and more comfortable life.

Medicare is high on the Liberal agenda because the system is sick and badly in need of resuscitation. Health Minister Monique Begin says that the system is threatened by extra
fees imposed by doctors and by hospitals that levy user fees.
Begin says that in the last four years charges "went out of
control and we don't know about the future."[1]

The doctors express different concerns. The Canadian

Medical Association, representing 37,000 doctors, says that one obvious symptom of Medicare's illness is the long wait for hospital beds in some provinces. CMA president Dr. Marc Baltzan estimated there are now 150,000 Canadians waiting for hospital beds, and in Newfoundland patients wait from two to two and a half years for eye surgery or to have hips replaced.[2]

Doctors and government alike want to save Medicare but they disagree vehemently on the remedy. The only consensus is that the problem is money. Beyond that, the dispute revolves around whether it should be the federal or the provincial governments, or the patients themselves, who pick up the tab for the shortfall. One great advantage of a well-run economy, operating at or near capacity, would be higher revenues for both federal and provincial governments, which would facilitate resolution of a problem that is really an offspring of the recession.

The Canadian pension system is also crying out for attention. The present hodgepodge is grossly unfair. Some people are in line for three, four, or more pensions while others only qualify for one. In addition, the privileged have their pensions indexed while the majority do not. The Canadian Labour Congress and others have called for widespread reform. The range of suggestions includes greater adequacy, universal indexing, provision for housewives, earlier vesting, and more portability. The number of permutations and combinations on the table is endless.

Progress has been slowed to a snail's pace by the recession. It is extremely difficult to build an adequate system on a foundation of uncertainty. The retroactive indexation of private plans would impose an enormous burden on them. Concern has also been expressed about the actuarial liability of public plans which is increasing at such a staggering rate there is doubt about the ability of future generations to pay.

The elimination of inflation would be a good starting point because with it goes the need for indexation—one of the current bones of contention. The whole pension problem becomes less complex and more manageable in a stable environment. Canada needs a fully funded, fully vesting, and fully portable system to replace the existing mosaic. A strong, dynamic economy would facilitate the transition to something of that kind.

I have already discussed the potential impact of low interest rates on home ownership—a subject close to my heart. A financial system free from the distortions caused by inflation would make it possible for any average income Canadian to buy a house if he or she wanted one. The rest of the good news is that low interest rates would be just as beneficial to renters as buyers. In most areas the problem is not so much a physical shortage of housing as it is of affordability. Rents are just too high for many pensioners, single parents, and the working poor. So their only recourse is to line up for public or subsidized housing of some sort and the queue is getting longer with the passing months.

Interest rates of the kind we enjoyed in the 1950s would reduce existing rentals by approximately half. This would eliminate the necessity of rent controls as a volume of new low-cost construction came on the market. It would also sharply reduce the need for public housing because the industry would again be in a position to meet the needs of the majority.

Pollution control is another issue that should be

addressed with wartime efficiency and dispatch. What a tragedy that many of Ontario's finest beaches were closed to bathing for most of the summer in 1983—the hottest summer in memory. The fecal coliform counts were too high to meet the rigorous tests of health regulations.

It is equally ironic that, at a time when our American neighbors are finally treating the question of acid rain seriously, we should be dragging our feet on the kind of action that would act as a spur. Until we can point to dramatic improvement with our major pollutors like the INCO smelting plant at Sudbury and Ontario Hydro's big coal-fired generator at Nanticoke, our bargaining power will be minimal. Only by showing the way can we hope to prod the Americans on.

In the end it doesn't really matter very much how the cost is shared between the companies and governments. Ultimately, we all pick up the check *in toto*, whether as consumers or taxpayers. The important point is not to let arguments over cost-sharing postpone these urgent remedial works. We are all winners if we act now. By next spring another lake may be dead.

A plea to get on with the megaprojects may seem out of place in a schedule of social concerns, but that judgment could be hasty. We need the plants to extract oil from the tar sands and the offshore drilling and pipelines to protect ordinary Canadians from the ravages of the next energy crisis, whenever it occurs. Foresight can pay big dividends somewhere down the line.

There is another reason for some of the projects and that is to give the Atlantic provinces the sort of economic shot in the arm that will spur their development and the diversification that will inevitably follow. Our Atlantic area has been endowed far beyond the dreams of its perennial optimists. The challenge is to press on and maximize the advantages from such rich resources.

Probably the most important problem requiring attention is the distribution of income and the elimination of debilitating poverty both in Canada and throughout the world. Justice is not guaranteed even when an economy is operating at its optimum, so some discussion of principles seems to be in order.

It is a fact that simple percentage increases in wages, based on the previous year's rise in real output per person, would exacerbate the present distribution of income that divides society into two classes: the fortunate who can well afford the five basic necessities (which in Canada include food, clothing, shelter, telephone, and television) and the poor who cannot. In addition, though less serious, is the fact that some historical wage relationship may be so badly out of joint as to be untenable. These must be adjusted for the sake of harmony.

Another discrepancy is the fact that the more powerful groups in society—managers, professionals, government employees, and workers in monopolistic and oligopolistic industries—enjoy fringe benefits far in excess of those provided to people in smaller, more competitive industry. People with market power take more holidays, receive better medical coverage, and enjoy bigger pensions than the population at large.

While historical pay relationships are significant and can't be ignored, an obvious dilemma arises from the fact that approximately 15 percent of our fellow citizens exist on

incomes that are well below the poverty line. These are the
people who cannot afford the basics and who rely, for survival, on subsidies of various sorts. My knowledge of their
plight comes not from reading books but from firsthand
experience with the problems of my electors.[3] My responsibility took me right into the heart of problemland, where many
of my friends paid 40 percent or more of their income for
shelter. Some were considering taking teen-age sons and
daughters out of high school because they couldn't afford the
shoes, clothes, and winter jackets essential for fast-growing
children.

These are only examples and by no means extreme. The
story goes on and on until the heart is weary and the mind
frustrated to the point of exasperation in trying to cope and
explain such poverty in an "affluent" society. The Report of
the Task Force on Housing and Urban Development, which I
had the honor to chair in 1968 – 69, put the situation more
poignantly than I can. It described the urban environment
this way: "Here too, is poverty in its rawest and ugliest form.
No pretty gardens or painted cottages here to camouflage
economic depression. Poverty in the worst areas of the city
core is abundantly visible in the decrepit structures which
form its housing, the cracked pavements of the streets which
are its recreational area, and the rodents which are its wild-
life. This poverty you can see—and hear—and taste—and
smell. Its residents are not simply families struggling to catch
up to the average national income; too often, they are people
fighting to retain a vestige of human dignity and self-respect.
No Task Force impression is more vivid of mind or depressing
of spirit than those found amid the blight and slum of Canada's larger cities."[4]

It is erroneous to assume that in conditions of full employment and stable prices the problem of poverty would slowly but inexorably disappear. The advantages would be very great, especially for people who could then get jobs in a full employment situation. But the arithmetic proves that with across-the-board percentage increases, the rich would still get richer and the poor get poorer, relatively speaking.

Figure 9 shows what happens when those with muscle, working for companies in a position to pass their higher costs on to the consumer, increase their share of the pie.

Figure 10 demonstrates what would happen in the relationship between someone earning a minimum wage of $3 and a neighbor earning $9 hourly if each salary increased at a compound rate of 3 percent for twenty years. The starting gap of $6 an hour spreads to $10.83 before the end of the century—from $240 to $433.20 for a forty-hour week. Quite obviously, the result would not be improved if each were compounded at a higher rate—say 7 percent.

People working at or near the minimum wage, who cannot afford to have faulty wiring or plumbing fixed or leaky roofs repaired, will be even worse off in the years ahead unless the trend is reversed.

Figure 10 illustrates the stark choice for society. Either the incomes policy must narrow the gap between workers at the bottom of the heap and their more fortunate brothers, or else society must accept the consequences of a class system in which the majority earn more than enough to pay their own way, while the minority comprising the "working poor" never will.

There has never been any doubt in my mind as to which route is correct. It is really a matter of human dignity.

Figure 9
Comparison of Transportation and Clothing Workers' Wages, 1968 – 1980

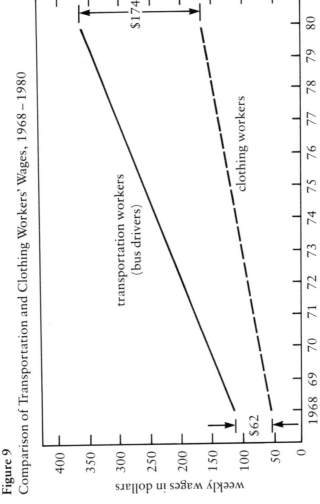

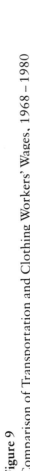

Source: Labor Canada: "Wage Rates, Salaries and Hours of Labor."

Nobody should be forced to rely on subsidies and handouts. Yet, if the incomes attached to some jobs are below the subsistence level, there is no other choice. Happily, the morally preferable solution is also the most economic.

After a lifetime in politics, I have become skeptical about the efficiency of bureaucratic machines in handing out subsidies, food stamps, and other goodies. Some social workers are entirely too paternalistic and condescending. And they, too, have to be paid. Consequently, the redistribution of income through wages, where the mechanics are already in place, has to be at least several percentage points less costly than collecting money through taxes and then mailing checks to the unfortunate minority.

Figure 10

Projection of Minimum and Skilled Tradesmen's Wages, 1980 – 2000

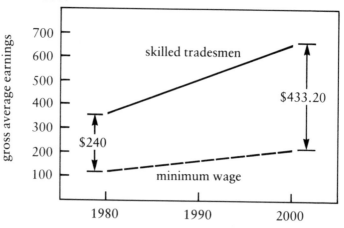

Let me make it perfectly clear that I am not suggesting income equality. There are differences of skill, risk, and discomfort among jobs. But more compelling is the fact that there is not, never has been, and probably never will be a society of any size that practices wage parity. There is always a pecking order, and as long as people are people, incentives will remain important—a touch of the American dream. At the same time there is no justification for incomes below the poverty line—especially when they could be brought up to the essential minimum over a reasonable period without any significant sacrifice on the part of either the rich or the middle classes.

It is not for me to prescribe the precise mechanics. But in principle, guidelines should be set in such a way that the relative position of workers at the bottom end of the pay scale, compared to average industrial wages and tradesmen's wages, should steadily improve. Bluntly stated, if tradesmen get a 10-cent-an-hour increase, people below the poverty line should get 12 cents. And while these figures are only by way of illustration, the point must be clearly made that the income gap between those whose services are most in demand and those of citizens who are in greatest need of their services must not widen, either relatively or absolutely. In a prolifically affluent society with a good potential for further growth, the numbers of both families and individuals with incomes below a generally accepted poverty line should continue to shrink. This is a social goal with widespread support, at least in theory. But satisfactory progress can never be achieved until the current vogue of across-the-board percentage increases is renounced—a fundamental change of attitude requiring trade-union initiative backed by enlightened public support.

The redistribution of income within the union movement is a problem that union people are well qualified to adjudicate. Weighing conflicting claims in the balance might not be a comfortable vocation, but it would be an essential service that would quickly expose any glaring inconsistencies between rhetoric and arithmetic.

It would remain to politicians to address the problem of determining those fringe benefits that might reasonably apply to all citizens rather than just the privileged and powerful. All groups in society pay the cost of the benefits that have been accumulated by both professional and labor groups with market power. There is no reason why the population at large should not enjoy an extended range of comparable benefits. But it is important to remember that fringe benefits, too, cost money. So the cost of an extension of these by means of legislation has to be deducted from the total increment of real wealth available for distribution in the form of higher wages. Otherwise, the tender balance between real output and real rewards would be upset.

Not only do we have to address the problem of internal poverty and distribution of income; we must become increasingly sensitive to world poverty and the growing gap between Old and New World incomes. That issue, too, must be squarely faced. It seems callous for us to be talking of a thirty-hour week while millions die of malnutrition and disease.

Happily, the plan I propose would be a godsend for poor countries. For most of them the number-one problem is selling enough goods for cash to pay the interest on their enormous debt. They are running on a treadmill, just standing still or slipping backward. Low interest rates would cut their debt payments in half and leave a surplus for other essential purposes.

Then the return of full employment in the West would increase demand for a whole range of primary products like hemp and cocoa. Higher prices would likely follow, and these offer a more realistic prospect of greater income for developing countries than reliance on ineffective cartels as proposed under the "New Economic Order."

There would be other benefits. It is very difficult, politically, to lower tariff barriers in a policy of "trade instead of aid" when unemployment is high and workers are threatened. Votes and principles clash. When everyone is working, however, higher quotas of foreign goods can be absorbed with a minimum of fuss. Similarly, aid allocations can be increased substantially with scarcely a murmur of dissent.

There is a parallel between the problems of domestic poverty and redistribution and their gargantuan international counterpart. Both are easier to attack when the economy is growing and employment high than when the opposite is true. This is an observation based on long years of political experience—and, after all, it is political economy we are talking about, not just abstract theory. Politicians find it far more convenient to distribute increments of increased output than to increase taxes and take income away from people who are conditioned to having it.

It may be difficult for some of my Liberal friends to believe that I have been talking about practical possibilities and not just idle dreams. They might well ask why, if the remedy is so straightforward, it hasn't been put into effect long ago. In reply I can only say that the human mind is not as open to new ideas as we pretend.

In the middle of the nineteenth century Ignaz Semmelweiss, a Hungarian doctor practicing in Vienna, was deeply concerned by the number of female patients dying from childbed fever. Eventually, the solution became clear to him and he wrote a paper for discussion with his colleagues. They were incensed. Instead of granting his request for a controlled experiment, his superior reminded him that they were university graduates and not willing to be insulted by his simplistic solution. They took away Semmelweiss' license to practice and he spent the rest of his days a disillusioned and despondent man.

Ten years later Lister and his team of British doctors authenticated Semmelweiss' discovery, which was simply that doctors and students were carrying the disease from patient to patient and from cadavers to live patients because they did not wash their hands in between examinations. Meanwhile, in the intervening years, thousands of women in hospitals all across Europe died unnecessarily because learned men were either too proud or too stubborn to admit that they might have overlooked the obvious.

I keep wondering how many more innocent people will lose their jobs, homes, farms, and maybe their self-respect before our learned economists catch up, once again, with reality.

I have tried to convey some of the passion I feel about the necessity of making our system work not just adequately but well—for the betterment of all mankind. To repeat the final paragraph of an earlier attempt, "I believe that rational change can best take place in a decentralized society where

man, not the State, is supreme. Rational change will permit
us to keep our basic freedoms, and to add those new ones
necessary to enchance our quality of life. Full employment
and stable prices will give us the maximum range of choice
with which to assert equality of opportunity and justice for
all. This is the liberalism I espouse. It is not a liberalism of the
left or of the right but, I believe, a rational and, above all,
humane liberalism."[5]

NOTES

1 *Toronto Star*, August 29, 1983, p. 1.
2 *Ibid*.
3 As member of Parliament for Davenport, 1949 – 57, and Trinity,
   1958 – 74 (both working-class ethnic districts of Toronto).
4 The Task Force on Housing and Urban Development was
   established by the federal government in August 1968. Its report
   was published the following spring.
5 PAUL T. HELLYER, *Agenda: A Plan for Action* (Scarborough,
   Ontario: Prentice-Hall of Canada, Ltd., 1971), pp. 205 – 06.

Bibliography

ACKLEY, GARDNER. *Macroeconomic Theory.* New York: The Macmillan Company, 1973.

ASHLEY, SIR WILLIAM. ed. *Principles of Political Economy.* New York: Augustus M. Kelly publishers, 1909.

BAIRD, CHARLES W. *Macroeconomics: An Integration of Monetary Search and Incomes Theories.* Los Angeles: University of California, 1978.

Bank of Canada, *1980 Report.* Ottawa, March 1981.

BEIGIE, CARL E. *Inflation is a Social Malady.* U.K.: British North American Committee, March 1979.

CLINTON, KEVIN, and KEVIN LYNCH. *Monetary Base and Money Stock in Canada.* Bank of Canada, Technical Report, July 16, 1979.

Conference Board Economic Forum, Inflation in the United States. *Causes and Consequences.* New York: 1974.

Congress of the United States. *Domestic Oil Prices: An Overview.* May 1979, Congressional Budget Office, Washington, D.C.

Congress of the United States. *The Economic Outlook for 1979–80, An Update.* A Report to the Senate and House Committees on the Budget, 1979.

Congress of the United States. "Energy, A Stubborn Component of Inflation." *Congressional Quarterly*, 1975.

Congress of the United States. *Five-Year Budget Projections and Alternative Budget Strategies for Fiscal Years 1980–84, Supplemental Report on Tax Expenditures*, 1979.

CROZIER, ROBERT B. *Deficit Financing and Inflation: Facts and Fictions.* Ottawa: The Conference Board of Canada, March 1973.

217

DORFMAN, ROBERT. *The Price System*. New York: Prentice-Hall, 1964.

Economic Report of the President together with The Annual Report of the Council of Economic Advisers, January 1962, 1974, 1978, 1979, 1980, 1981, and February 1971, 1982 and 1983.

Executive Office of the President. *A Quarterly Report of the Council on Wage and Price Stability*, April 1978.

FRIEDMAN, MILTON. *The Counter-Revolution in Monetary Theory*. London: Institute of Economic Affairs, 1970.

. *Indexing and Inflation*. Washington: American Enterprise Institute for Public Policy Research, 1974.

. *Inflation: Causes and Consequences*. London: Asia Publishing House, 1963.

. *Inflation and Unemployment: The New Dimension of Politics*. London: Institute of Economic Affairs, 1977.

. *A Program for Monetary Stability*. New York: Fordham Press, 1960.

, and Rose D. Friedman. *Free to Choose*. New York: Avon Books, 1981.

GALBRAITH, JOHN K. *The Affluent Society*. Boston: Houghton Mifflin and Company, 1976.

. *The New Industrial State*. Boston: Houghton Mifflin and Company, 1971.

. *Money—Whence It Came, Where It Went*. Boston: Houghton Mifflin and Company, 1975.

GILDER, GEORGE. *Wealth and Poverty*. New York: Basic Books, Inc. 1981.

HARRISS, C. LOWELL, ed. *Inflation: Long-Term Problems*. New York: The Academy of Political Science in conjunction with the Lehrman Institute, 1975.

HEILBRONER, ROBERT L. *Beyond Boom and Crash*. New York: W. W. Norton and Company, Inc., 1978.

, and LESTER C. THUROW. *The Economic Problem*. Englewood Cliffs, N.J.: Prentice-Hall, Inc., 1975.

HELLER, WALTER. *The Economy, Old Myths and New Realities*. W. W. Norton and Company, Inc., 1976.

HELLYER, PAUL T. *Agenda: A Plan for Action*. Toronto: Prentice-Hall of Canada Ltd., 1971.

HOFSTADTER, RICHARD. *The Age of Reform*. Northhampton, Great Britain: John Dickens and Conner Ltd., 1962.

JONES, AUBREY. *The New Inflation: The Politics of Prices and Incomes*. Penguin Books Inc., 1973.

KAHN, HERMAN. *World Economic Development, 1979 and Beyond*. Boulder, Colorado: Westview Press, 1979.

KEYNES, J. M. *The General Theory of Employment, Interest and Money*. London: Macmillan and Co. Ltd., and New York: St. Martin's Press, Inc., 1960.

LEKACHMAN, ROBERT. *Inflation: The Permanent Problem of Boom and Bust*. New York: Vintage Books, 1973.

LOW, RICHARD E., ed. *The Economics of Antitrust, Competition and Monopoly*. Englewood Cliffs, N.J.: Prentice-Hall, Inc., 1968.

MCCRACKEN, PAUL, and a group of independent experts. *Towards Full Employment and Price Stability*. The Organization for Economic Cooperation and Development, 1977.

MEGAW, W.J., ed. *Prospects for Man: Economics, Inflation and Unemployment*, A symposium presented by the Faculty of Science, York University.

MORRISON, ROBERT S. *Inflation Can Be Stopped*. Cleveland, Ohio: Western Reserve Press, 1973.

NOVAK, MICHAEL. *The Spirit of Democratic Capitalism*. New York: Simon and Schuster, 1982.

O.E.C.D., *Economic Outlook*, July 1979.

O.E.C.D., *Main Economic Indicators*, December 1979.

O.E.C.D., *National Accounts of OECD Countries*, 1976.

O.E.C.D., *Labour Force Statistics*, 1965–76.

OKUN, ARTHUR, ed. *The Battle Against Unemployment*. New York: W. W. Norton and Company, Inc., 1972.

OKUN, ARTHUR M., and GEORGE L. PERRY, *Curing Chronic Inflation* Washington, D.C.: The Brookings Institute, 1978.

PALMER, JOHN L. *Creating Jobs: Public Employment Programs and Wage Subsidies*. Washington, D.C.: The Brookings Institute, 1978.

. *Inflation, Unemployment and Poverty*. Lexington, Mass: Lexington Books, 1973.

PETERSON, WALLACE C. *Income, Employment and Economic Growth*. New York: W. W. Norton and Company, Inc., 1978.

SAMUELSON, PAUL A. *Economics*, 9th ed. New York: McGraw-Hill Book Company, 1973.

SIMON, WILLIAM E. *A Time for Truth*. New York: McGraw-Hill Book Company, 1978.

SMITH, ADAM. *Wealth of Nations*. London: Methuen and Co., 1964.

THUROW, LESTER C. *The Zero-Sum Society*. New York: Basic Books, 1980.

. *Dangerous Currents: The State of Economics*. New York: Random House, Inc., 1983.

TREVITHICK, JAMES ANTHONY, and CHARLES MULVEY. *The Economics of Inflation*. New York: John Wiley and Sons, Inc., 1975.

United Kingdom, *Parliamentary Debates*, Vol. CLXXXII.

United States Department of Commerce. *Historical Statistics of the United States, Colonial Times to 1970*, Bureau of Census, Part 2.

United States Department of Commerce, 1972 Census of Manufactures. *Concentration Ratios in Manufacturing.* 1975.

United States Department of Commerce. *Statistical Abstracts of the United States.* Bureau of the Census, 1977.

United States Department of Commerce, Survey of Current Business, *Inflation and Unemployment.* Congressional Quarterly Inc., 1975.

United States Department of Commerce, Survey of Current Business, *The Economy in 1970.* January 1979.

United States Department of Commerce, Survey of Current Business, *National Income Issue*, Bureau of Economic Analyses, January 1976, Volume 56, No 1, Part II.

United States Department of Energy. *National Energy Plan II, A Report to Congress*, May 1979.

United States Department of Labor, Bureau of Labor Statistics. *Handbook of Labor Statistics* 1977 and *Monthly Labor Review*, September 1978.

United States Bureau of Public Affairs. *Multinational Corporations*, September 1978.

WALLICH, HENRY C., and MABEL I. WALLICH. "What Have We Learned About Inflation," *Challenge Magazine*, March/April 1973.

WANNISKI, JUDE. "The Mundell-Laffer Hypothesis, A View of the World Economy," *The Public Interest*, No 39, Spring 1975.

WEINTRAUB, SIDNEY. *Capitalism's Inflation and Unemployment Crisis.* New York: Addison-Wesley Publishing Company, Inc., 1978.

———. "Wall Street's Mindless Affair with Tight Money," *Challenge Magazine*, January/February 1978.

The Author

One of Canada's most prominent and controversial political figures, Paul Hellyer has been actively involved in public affairs since 1949, and has held senior cabinet portfolios under prime ministers St. Laurent, Pearson, and Trudeau. He now contributes a regular column to the *Toronto Sun*, and is a much sought-after public speaker.